Di

F. de Kirchner

Clarososcuros biography of
Argentina President

Joaquín Abad

Joaquín Abad

Discovering Cristina Kirchner

Joaquín Abad

DEDICATION

The writing team that years ago agglutinated Rafael M. Bernaldo de Quirós to take online magazine People, whose numbers, enriched come to light now in printed book format, under the guise of discovering.

Joaquín Abad

ARGUMENT

The president of the Argentina nation with the highest personal wealth in Latin America, has a full biography full of chiaroscuro that make a real eyesore. A life full of passionate affairs with young men whom he has elevated to high positions of the Argentine government and that qualify as a true "assault cribs". Some suicide not clarified and many contradictions of a friend president of Chavismo hiding untold fortune of tens of billions of dollars in dollars, gold and other precious materials, in the vault of his mansion in Calafate, apart from what saved in banks Swiss and other tax havens. She dresses black widow when it is common knowledge that for many, many years, the relationship with her husband, Nestor Kirchner, It was only apparent because each had their romantic relationships ... just they kept a society for enrichment limit. It is known bags full of dollars often transported from the Casa Rosada to Calafate. It is known multibillion clandestine contributions of multinationals both their election campaigns as their personal fortune.

But in Argentina all these economic and sexual scandals, which are public, serve only to the population in chronic MOFE and books ... Justice is subject to political power and judges filed and filed successive complaints of illicit enrichment while stunned voters contemplate the new "Evita" that governs a rich and great country

Joaquín Abad

without meeting his ministers ... they suffer ridicule Cristina interventions when manifested in international forums failing to ask some discomfort. As Chavez as other neighboring dictators, Cristina tries to amend the constitution and remain in power. It is a great example of the unpresentable which can be a character who rules a nation.

CHIAROSCURO A PRESIDENT

He relieved her husband Nestor Kirchner as president of Argentina in 2007 in an operation planned to be simultaneous continuity in office every eight years, deadline continuity in the presidency of the nation. Until that date was always the wife who accompanied the president into action. The support of the husband team in the election campaign made victorious by 28 October to the death of Nestor Kirchner just three years later of a suspected heart attack, looked as if they shared the presidency and was not unaware that although officially Cristina was the president, who pulled the strings was her husband, who accumulated power throughout the party apparatus, Front for Victory, and the government.

PARALLEL LIVES

As for their private lives, many years, many were only family law, not of fact. Both had their consensual extramarital affairs. They were like a company of two partners who hoarded a huge fortune thanks to the power and political charges since they formed couple amass proposed. And after going through the presidency of the nation Argentina riches multiplied by a thousand without any judge managed to initiate proceedings for illicit enrichment. Argentines seem to agree, again and again, politicians use their power to become millionaires immensely, because judges are appointed by parliament and all are outstanding not to upset the politicians who sponsor.

GRANDDAUGHTER OF IMMIGRANTS SPANISH

Cristina Elisabet Fernández Wilhelm was born on February 19, 1953 in the province of Buenos Aires, descendant of Galician father and mother of German descent. She was the daughter of a single mother for two years. After Bachiller he began studying psychology abandoned the law in La Plata, where he met Nestor Kirchner with which married in March 1975. After the coup the military in March 1976 decided to move to Rio Gallegos, which began the career in a law office. It is in Rio Gallegos where the couple begins making business, thanks to legal knowledge, with significant real estate.

In 1983 returns to Argentina democracy and Kirchner decided to bet on achieving political career Néstor be mayor of Rio Gallegos in 1987 and Cristina provincial congressman from the Justicialista Party, Peronist inspiration.

From there it was continually occupying increasingly important positions until his promotion culminates achieved thanks to her husband, the president of Argentina in 2007.

ILLICIT ENRICHMENT

Political activity Nestor-Cristina marriage has been accompanied by a dramatic enrichment that although many sources presumed illicit origin of the judges never prosecutes, under pressure of political power or unspeakable rewards.

Throughout these years the news of dismissal of cases against the Kirchners are continuous: Oyarbide dismissed the Kirchners in the cause for illicit enrichment, head which is described in great detail as a federal judge after meetings with senior decides to shelve one of the many lawsuits against the current president of the nation. Another thing is when Cristina longer be president, then federal judges will no such qualms and the truth will come to light, as is usual in Argentina with performances by previous presidents. Right now the debate is on the supposed building a strong -box vault similar to using the benches in the villa that the Kirchners have in Calafate where supposedly thousands of dollars are saved in cash. As the end of the second term of Cristina in front of Argentina are coming to light alleged corruption approaches. Even it filed a complaint by the Justicialist Juan Ricardo Mussa, who says Nestor Kirchner was actually shot dead in the head after a heated argument with his wife, President, and that the death was disguised attack. Now ask the body is exhumed to check the veracity of information from witnesses who claim that he was killed. The Ercoli judge must decide whether to accept the demand. Nestor Kirchner who says he actually was killed shot in the head after a heated argument with his wife, President, and that the death was disguised attack. Now ask the body is exhumed to check the veracity of information from witnesses who claim that he was killed. The Ercoli judge must decide whether to accept the demand. Nestor Kirchner who says he actually was killed shot in the head after a heated argument with his wife, President, and that the death was disguised attack. Now ask the body is exhumed to check the veracity of information from witnesses who claim that he was killed. The Ercoli judge must decide whether to accept the demand.

In any case already holds press the number of businessmen linked to politicians in corruption cases dotting the Kirchners, who stopped not ask millionaire contributions to companies for their election campaigns and witnesses who now make memory and have the luggage with millions who were taken from Rosara mansion House to the Kirchners in Calafate. On television that fails to silence lovers Interviewing Cristina Nestor secretaries, architects with blueprints of the mansion in Calafate where the vault was built. We are witnessing the beginning of the end of a presidency riddled with corruption and chiaroscuro, with large doses of infidelity and love affairs, both Nestor and Cristina, the latter with the former Spanish judge Baltasar Garzon, several years younger than her years.

THE FORBIDDEN HISTORY

Eduardo Fernandez, father of Cristina, is hidden from the public figure, and that the president was responsible for burying his story in the darkest depths of ignorance.

Perfil newspaper investigated this issue a few years ago truly amazing drawing conclusions because "those who know that stage of life Cristina ensure that (actually) felt somewhat ashamed of their parents. Why he sought to reinvent its history, obviating part of his past. He wants to control everything, in fact if for her, her life would start at 22 ".

And it is strange that avoid going to La Plata, where he spent much of his childhood and adolescence, and displayed so cold and aloof in public with her mother, Ofelia Wilhelm, and his younger sister, Giselle. What hides Cristina? What about your family? What does his father in the life of the president?

The son of one of the partners who worked with Fernandez told the newspaper Profile: "I met a couple of years Cristina Lujan ago. Thrilled I went to tell my father, my brother and I had worked with his father, who was an excellent person. She did not even flinch. He did not say a word. I was surprised by her coldness, I thought as any of us would like to be reminded of his father ".

Known as the "red" or "co-co" by his stammer, the father of the president-elect, son of Spanish immigrants, bought half of a group of Expreso City Bell with help from their parents, and became chauffeur line linking the town with La Plata. Despite facing 14-hour days, "the Colorado was not afraid to work, although it is also true that Young liked nightlife and had success with women. Yes, it was super responsible, always on time and if it had come out, and it showed "recalls one of the employees.

Fernandez became owner of three groups, elected chief of staff, a position he held until his death on April 26, 1982, leaving a series of questions about the life of Cristina unresolved. "It was a strange house, there was never a relaxed atmosphere. Except Giselle, who lived all that away because of his innocence, Ofelia, Eduardo and Cristina were more independent. Who all lived under the same roof was a mere circumstance "said a person close to the family person.

Ofelia Cristina and her father practically ignored, but Giselle always welcomed with open arms. It seems that the origin of this situation is that the mother became pregnant with the president before formalizing its relationship with Eduardo, which was a social scandal, "Ofelia could never forget those early years of solitude with her daughter. Cristina could never get over the feeling that his birth had not been programmed, "says a relative.

"Cristina disowned his family. Sometimes I feel that she was embarrassed. He resented the poor neighborhood where they lived, the house decorated with plastic flowers and porcelain animals ... The fanaticism bothered his mother for football, and the simplicity of its colectivero father. Therefore, from adolescence, he began to build itself and tried to break away from his past. "

And while he did, Cristina Kirchner managed to outrun Fernandez and create a whole aura of skepticism about its origin, which would lay the foundation of his person, which has become president-elect of Argentina

known love of the President of Argentina

Almost seven out of ten Argentines voted to occupy the famous Casa Rosada, but it looks like a dark past into question the Kirchners, even with former President underground.

The couple agreed at the time that each could have lovers is in the public domain, but we still escape various subterfuges which was the most consistent marriage of Argentina society.

Cristina has become the most powerful woman in the history of their country becoming itself, building a story that clearly seems to be far removed from reality. On his personal story follows an absolute secrecy, although being born died shortly Eva Duarte de Peron is one of those coincidences that makes us think that our history is both whimsical.

Based on a hard life, Fernandez was forged as a sweeping and confident figure.

First boyfriend, first step towards high society

With the tender age of 16 had his first known Cristina boyfriend, rugby player Raul Cafferata, who introduced her to an unknown world for her, refined Jockey Club of La Plata.

Psychology was about to snatch Argentina to

the great lady of politics, but finally decided to study at the Faculty of Law at the National University of La Plata, where he began his political activism in Front of Groups Eva Peron, organization student linked to the Montoneros, a stain on the curriculum of the President.

It was in October 1974 when he met Nestor Kirchner, a union that became official Spring Day that year at a picnic in the park Pereyra. A day to remember, at least for Cristina Kirchner acknowledged as being drunk that day and not remember what he had done to woo Cristina.

A young Nestor long hair and glasses thick glass could access the cold heart of the President with his verve and, as indicated by the gossips, known and respected for his family. All this made the university, completely in love with the gawky Kirchner broke with Cafferata.

Fellow activists in the Peronist Youth, took just over six months in a civil marriage, namely in May 1975. A wedding there are no known photographs and whose honeymoon would in a pension until military coup of 24 March 1976 they returned to reality.

Before fleeing to Rio Gallegos, Santa Cruz, Nestor graduated while under Cristina continues to doubt if ever the tests performed credited as a lawyer. Several investigations suggest that the title would not be true, even though the authorities of the University of La Plata say it is.

Max, bear

On February 16, 1977 came into the world the first child of the couple, a child who, according to the president, had "easy character" but turned out to be a good student, as he tried to take off journalism and law but not concluded.

When Cristina already had 37 years of age born Florence, the darling of his father. A girl who grew up with an absent mother figure beside his father.

His relationship with Nestor has always been described as intense, in fact his wife left him in evidence on several occasions, as in the closure of one of the acts of the 2003 campaign, in which Kirchner spoke of nationalizing the railways. When he dined with his entourage, Cristina burst like a runaway horse in the room and badly told her husband that the idea "atrasaba" the country. An enraged Nestor angrily shouted: "Go away Santa Cruz and stop dammit!".

They even were on the verge of breaking at the end of 1981, according to his relatives commented: "It was the only time he could think of a divorce. Cristina was furious fear. He threatened to leave; but he convinced her, you could say that bowed. His private life was said that for a long time did not sleep together. Apparently they had reached an agreement through which each individually solve your love life. Cristina had her lovers, Nestor theirs. Other frontline officers claim that this was known ...

and suffered. Never really he did not take a genius to realize that the love between Nestor and Cristina had spent a long time: in the last 20 years there has never been public demonstrations of affection between the two. "

Cristina itself told his biographer: "We were not of us displays of affection in front of people." However, after his death, President Nestor cried many times on camera. And in the recent campaign speeches he was seen on several occasions, excited, with tears in his eyes. That feature of sensible, human, woman joined him a lot of female votes. "I do not know if I ever lied Nestor; and if I lied, and I will not find out. But what I'm sure is never bored me. I said it's also the only person that I was not bored. Since I met him until he died, Nestor made me. Laugh "

.

Judge Garzon, LAST LOVER CRISTINA

Was the Mexican magazine "Who" the first who dared to publish the news that former Spanish judge Baltasar Garzón (58 years) maintained a love affair with the president of Argentina, Cristina Fernandez (60), adding to the Spanish character the long list of known lovers president, with recognized reputation for "assails cots" as most of her lovers have been much younger than her. "Who" ensures that when Garzón and Fernandez agreed "the meeting of two such strong personalities became instant passion."

It has been the correspondent of the magazine in Madrid, Veronica Calderon, who signed the report where other lovers of the judge mentioned in Argentina, specifically with a

Brazilian and a Colombian. As is known, Baltasar Garzon, who if became famous in Spain after his stint as Magistrate Judge of the High Court, after passing through other trial courts in the provinces, have official residence in Argentina after the Supreme condemn him 9 February 2012 by prevarication. The President herself, Cristina, handed personally late last year an Argentine identity card, so the former judge now enjoys dual citizenship.

There are many times that both former judge and president, they have been together in official events since he was invited in 2011 to the inauguration of Cristina.

Those close to the Casa Rosada people have filtering is the president herself who has commissioned Baltasar Garzon to lead the legal reform in Argentina, for the own former judge has initiated a series of working contacts with leaders of the country to start such reform that has no other purpose than to submit further justice to political power. As we know, nothing known disqualification of the judge in Spain, Congress of Argentina hired him as a consultant to the Commission on Human Rights.

Idyll passionate about the Spanish press has humorously priming. As shown, the article signed by journalist Andrés Chaves canary in the newspaper "The Day" last March:

Pues, yes, the rabbit Risco me bitch. Baltasar Garzon, the Spanish judge prevaricating, may be living a passionate love affair with Argentina's President Cristina Kirchner. He says, for the glory of his mother, the Mexican magazine "Who", sold 82,000 copies that every time he goes to the street.

I recognize that I had noticed in the news, knowing glances between them like old lovers. But for love there is no age and there are also those who like to take refuge from wrinkles. Adolfo Dominguez has already said, in a moment of inspiration: "Wrinkles are beautiful". But Garzón did not see Adolfo Dominguez; in case of "La Martina" to make new homeland.

True to this rough trend, Baltasar, love hawk which has been launched against the widow of squint to see if fishing tremulous meat. And, by God, he did it, as long as the Mexican chronicles fly over Spain, Argentina, Mexico itself and emerging countries in which Garzón is a leader; probably because they do not know.

And the former judge and former bizco shared the same hobbies unearthing dead to shrivel inheritance, also called historical memory. Garzón opened graves, but only of the dead from one side of the Spanish Civil War; Ernesto Kirchner and those of the dead of Argentina, cruel, terrible, stupid and gloomy dictatorship. Do you remember also intervened - former judge against General Pinochet, who was persecuted by Garzón until the British authorities hunted in London-'m gorged of universal justice and sent the dictator to hell to

Santiago, then months in a golden cage. I would have gotten into the Tower of London in perpetuity, for bastard.

Cristina and Baltasar, like two lovers, attending various events together by the country of her; and she has given him, pledge, Argentine DNI. Then comes the Argentine driving license, passport and national membership card Polo Club of Buenos Aires; Later they will honor Porteno and as a corollary, will give an apartment in the Casa Rosada, so you can see more closely Hebe de Bonafini, Dona Rogelia version, heavier than Snow White's stepmother. I have never seen so much love bureaucratic identity cards. It is seen that themselves are rare, he and she.

Of course everyone has the right to fall in love. They say love is a crocodile in the river of desire; it must be because devours lovers. "Neither you without me, nor I without you," it seems to have whispered Cristina Fernández (ex Kirchner, let's speak clearly) to Balthazar ear. "Love me little, if you want to love me long," Garzón would have said, quoting Herrick. Ernesto Kirchner, from the grave, will be roared: "Is that just loved ever Many people have died, like me, who feels love yet," correcting a little quote from Balzac and chafándoles somewhat the metisaca .

Because I wanted you to share with me this Sunday amazement. According to the Network, the magazine "Who" published the news yesterday, with some reservations; reserves that have no other means the whole world, which give the thing done. The 13, a channel that has something to do COPE, picked him up Friday in its news. I do not know how she will be sitting spreading the news to "El País", which has exclusive things Garzón, as is public knowledge.

See if the issue is then confirmed and married, bringing Cristina (Fernandez) would give his Baltasar other official document unite its many membership cards: the marriage certificate. He eventually naming him president of Repsol. Oh my God.

Origins of fortune and enrichment

Purchases of land that would later become airports, oil concessions ... Many are the actions associated with the disputed marriage enrichment Kirchner, who went to live in a boarding house in the early days of their relationship to occupy the most coveted home country .

Specifically, the late president bought land at $ 50,000, which were sold shortly after nearly two and a half million dollars.

This land has been pointed out many times by his detractors as the big business of the presidential family, as the value of nearly 200 hectares was sold to the power of Santa Cruz around 70% of the funds that the province has in the Exterior.

The construction of an airport in these lands earned him $ 2,300,000 near Kirchner and, moreover, the Land Department of the municipality of El Calafate gave awards suspended without giving further explanations for its citizens, as former president He was behind this urban fabric.

"InEl CalafateThey sold the distribution of land to friends of power and selling it at a priceoffercut the chances that ordinary people can have a field, "said the media Dr. Alvaro de Lamadrid on the decision of the Prosecutor Natalia Mercado, on the written as judge and jury in a trial" clearly incompatible with its function every time one hand on it lies the causefiledby Lamadrid and herself is acquiring land at ridiculously low prices and is part of the troupe of power was aided by the gale of land scattered around theineffableMendez, "provincial deputy in Santa Cruz and close friend of Kirchner.

Throughout this monograph on Argentina President we will reeled other aspects that contributed to its enrichment, denounced many times, such as the Civic Coalition back in 2010, acquiring two million dollars.

In the court filing behavior of the couple with defined in Article 268 of the Penal Code which punishes any public official who for profit use for themselves or for a third party confidential data was purchased.

The complaint was filed by deputies Juan Carlos Morán, Juan Carlos Vega and Elsa Quiroz, and noted that Kirchner bought thetwo million dollarsin October 2008,"Knowing that it was theopportune time to do sosince after the currency would increase its contribution. "

"This presumes that such conduct was carried out under theinformation sharing with President Cristina FernándezIn principle to be your spouse and also for being the political leader of the national government, "noted the report.

Cristina and speculation

The fact that, by its position, the president had inside information on market fluctuations could condition their enrichment at new levels, something that is evident, because in this particular case, Nestor Kirchner achieved an economic benefit but who He was ultimately enriched president Fernandez, as the profit advantage obtained a marriage Dower well.

the deceased former president had no choice but to recognize the purchase of two million dollars in October 2008 to acquire apackage of sharesa luxury hotel in the town of El Calafate, in Patagonia, southern Argentina. It was also noted that it would not be the only time that the marriage had played with speculation to increase their assets and thus invest in all types of businesses across the country.

If you do not understand this type of business carried out by marriage, beyond buying foreign exchange, October 1, 2008 the dollar exchange rate was 3.13 pesos, while 31 of the same month was the 3.37, resulting in a difference of 488,000 pesos (about $ 130,000 at current exchange rates) of exchange difference.

Enriching their relatives

In recent years, the Argentina press echoed the improvement of living standards of officials of the old and new "breed" of Kirchner stage. Luxury homes, cars and first-range urban properties that move millions of dollars a year. These are some of the most notorious cases:

Ricardo Echegaray, President of the Federal Administration of Public Revenue (AFIP)

He arrived in 2003 to Buenos Aires with assets of 168,650 pesos. After 10 years, he has 4'030.779 pesos. Your house is worth nearly two million pesos and has properties in Nordelta and springs, each valued at one million pesos.

Julio de Vido Minister of Federal Planning

It has a mansion called Puerto Panal, in Zárate. The country is in the name of his wife, has a lake, a riding stable and a soccer field.

RICARDO JAIME former Transportation Secretary

He does not represent many goods, but has a home in one of the most expensive places in Villa Carlos Paz, with private access to Lake San Roque. He has three houses on four sheets, each with a value of US $ 300 mil.

Health Minister Juan Manzur

Arriving in charge had as equity4'900.000 pesos. Four years later the figure rose to9000000and recently he bought a mansion in Yerba Buena. His house is valued at 6 million pesos.

DANIEL MUÑOZ former private secretary of Nestor Kirchner

In 2003, he had only one car as unique

heritage. Five years later he had a million pesos and now lives in a house more than a thousand square meters in an exclusive area in a Buenos Aires neighborhood.

Ricardo Barreiro charge of caring for the house Kirchner in El Calafate

It has a complex of cabins, a business collective, the granting of a shipping company and a restaurant in the city center. It Is Hotel Altos de Amaicha owner.

Fabian Gutierrez Secretary of Cristina Fernández

He began working for Nestor Kirchner in 2003. In five years its assets rose more than 58 thousand pesos to more than 402,000. It has a house overlooking the lake, pool, gym and worth a million dollars.

Rudy Ulloa former driver of Nestor Kirchner

It has a mansion in Rio Gallegos, the administration of two audiovisual production and high-end nine cars. It also has a luxury home in Las Lomas de San Isidro valued at 700 thousand dollars.

RAUL COPETTI Finance Manager Kirchner

In 2010 he acquired a land of 800 thousand dollars, where he built a complex of buildings and shops. It also has several hectares on the border between Junin and San Martin de los Andes.

NÉSTOR Periotti Director of National Roads and Highways

He bought a mansion for nearly two million occupying about 1,400 square meters.

Héctor Icazuriaga Head of the Secretariat of Intelligence

He bought a luxury apartment in the tower El Faro in Puerto Madero. From 2003 to 2013 its assets grew from73,995 pesosto1'681.964 pesos.

FRANCISCO LARCHER Secretary for
Intelligence

Homeowner in April, Berazategui, country valued at one million pesos.

He bought a five-hectare farm in the country Puerto Panal on behalf of one of its partners. According to the complaint, a record expenses9,000 pesos a month.

Judgments dismissed

It seems that justice has always protected the Kirchners, although the question of illicit enrichment has flown over the couple from their first steps in national politics.

Oyarbide, known judge who dared to cross the path of political dependence and dismiss allegations of officials "kirchneristas" dismissed an alleged illicit enrichment of the couple offense based on the statement of personnel manager Cristina Fernandez and Nestor Kirchner, Victor Manzanares, which he tried to explain the origin of assets increased $ 7,824,941 to marriage from $ 46,036,711.

Despite the dismissal, it calls attention to the heading of the document lodged the headquarters be set at a different province which should be in Capital Federal.

Neither has been able to clarify why were not

represented by a professional enrolled in the Bar Association of Capital Federal, for none of the partners is recorded in it, even though his defense as valid considered, so much so, that Oyarbide considered his dismissal.

Neither the prosecutor, Eduardo Taiano, nor his partner in the Office of Administrative Investigations (FIA), Guillermo Naoilles, had enough guts to appeal the judge's ruling, on which the plaintiff attorney, Enrique Piragini, it does have a few words: "the judge never summoned to appear tenants paying disproportionate amounts of rents, nor established the veracity of the supporting documents for accounting entries. It was a premature dismissal "of a complaint lodged in July 2009, based on the information that came off marriage as to increase its assets by more than 150%.

The judge in question

While the "shadow power" as regards his

enemies Cristina, I do not hesitate to make a move, and the Federal Court was denounced by illegal discharge of their duties by sobreseer the presidential couple.

To be supported, the president submitted an affidavit to the Office of Anticorruption, for the period filed the last day of 2009, since, like the previous year, underwent significant growth, although less than the previous year, of about 20% from above 46 million to over 55 million.

The focus is fixed this time in the cancellation of debts millions chasing the presidential couple. "I think the misrepresentation contained in the affidavits are an insignificant offense against the possible commission of crimes of influence peddling, bribery, money laundering of illicit origin and taxation and tax evasion," he declared Piragini at that time.

Given the unusual look of his detractors, Cristina was favored by the Anticorruption Office (OA), which for the first time in its history, ordered a second extension in the time period in which officials to develop their sworn financial disclosure.

"The privilege granted by OA to Cristina Kirchner and his officials, is to hide assets that have or to hide a shame we do not know if they have?" He declared indignantly gubernatorial candidate of the Frente Amplio Progresista, Margarita Estolbizer, who also He demanded the "immediate" resignation of the head of that office.

Marriage, who came to the Executive in 2003, managed to increase their wealth in just six years by more than 700%, resulted in $ 55.5 according to official documents available to the OA.

Previous sobreseimientos

Rodolfo Canicoba Corral is another name that more headaches brought Cristina Fernandez de Kirchner at the time, although just failing in their favor and her husband, the latter covered by the exemption from action by his death .

This judge took advantage in the record to dismiss the cause of alleged illicit enrichment, which began in 2008 by the complaint of lawyer Ricardo Monner Sans.

The only explanation given is that the dismissal was caused by "over time" because why is due to continue the investigation "no new evidence incorporated".

Even before this case, between 1995 and

2004, the couple was investigated for its heritage, closed shortly after Judge Julian Ercolini by.

What is clear is that he has never known, and it seems that will not be known, the heritage of the presidential couple, and now the Cristina widow, even protected by judges and the Federal Chamber itself, wrapped in an aura of mystery and uncertainty .

Environment under suspicion

Isidoro Bounine, private secretary Cristina, was under investigation for illicit enrichment, like his other three colleagues who worked for the president.

Young, 31, was in charge of bringing the phone to Kirchner, and even traveled with her and handled her account on the social network Twitter. 13 years ago that Bounine met the Kirchners in Santa Cruz, being hired as presidential secretary in 2005. That year he reported having $ 15,000 cash, however, this amount rose to $ 830,254 in just three years. In addition, it has been known that bought a house for his brother when his salary is only $ 14,282 monthly.

Bonadío he considered dismiss the case based on a report of the Body of Accounting Experts of the Court, in which it claimed that increased this fortune was "justified". Your personal situation has also played in his favor, because he is unmarried, has no children and their costs are minimal.

This is the second investigation presidential secretary and dismissed illicit enrichment, after the same judge shut a case against Daniel Alvarez, but are still suspected former officials Fabian Gutierrez and Hector Daniel Muñoz, the latter strongly criticized for spending to have a $ 14,000 account for more than one million in just four years.

Mil21.es published this information on the president.

Confirm the processing conspiracy and the seizure of $ 10.000 million against Cristina

Another legal setback for Senator-elect Cristina Kirchner. The Constitutional Court of the Federal Court of Cassation confirmed the prosecution for conspiracy and defrauding the State against former President Bachelet and seizure of 10,000 million pesos Judge Julián Ercolini, locked him in the case investigating the diversion of funds public works, in favor of Lázaro Báez.

The judges rejected a defense request of Senator like two applications lodged by the K entrepreneur -beneficiado with $ 46,000 million- millionaire complaining though. It is one of the most emblematic cases of corruption K.

Cristina back next to the Courts of Comodoro

Py to testify in another case that links with Lázaro Báez -preso laundering assets- week. It is not a simple scenario: Justice confirmed the prosecution for conspiracy and defrauding the state, as well as the seizure of 10,000 million pesos on its assets, ordered in the case investigating the diversion of funds from the highway public works in favor of Austral group.

The Constitutional Court of Cassation composed of judges Gustavo Hornos and Mariano Hernán Borinsky, turned down a presentation by the lawyer Carlos Beraldi defender of the former President, which opposed the confirmation processing performed in September, the Court of the Federal chamber Porteña, about Cristina Kirchner, Julio De Vido, Jose Lopez, Carlos Kirchner (cousin of former president) and the employer Lazaro Baez, among other defendants.

In the case in which prosecutors participated Gerardo Pollicita and Ignacio Mahiques addressing investigated through "multiple administrative irregularities", 52 highway contracts for 46,000 million pesos for the Southern Group. Aggravating is that 50% of the works were not completed, according to the record, and premiums were around 65% of the original value of the tenders.

Increasingly closer to being elevated to trial, the record defendants are accused of integrating a "conspiracy" between 2004-2015, was devoted to "commit crimes to seize unlawfully and intentionally funds allocated to the highway public works in Santa Cruz ". The contracts had a single recipient: Lázaro Báez. The "head" of the partnership, for justice, was Cristina Kirchner.

In addition, the judges of Cassation rejected two requests for the defense of the Southern Group was also confirmation complaint processing and the millionaire owner embargo. Thus, they gave confirmed the indictment for conspiracy as precautionary measure for 10,000 million pesos.

Recently, the prosecutor Pollicita requested more than 180 properties of all defendants in the case on corruption in public works, including Senator Citizen Unity, pass into the hands of justice as part of the seizure of 10,000 million pesos dictations in this investigation. In addition, opening safes Julio De Vido, Jose Lopez and the former President was asked.

The measure on the properties requested in order to prevent "deterioration that conspires against the equity guarantee occur," and why prosecutors asked that the kidnapping and judicial deposit "of registrable movable property becomes available.

Processing confirmed by the Federal Court and had his backing in the highest court in criminal matters, accused the former president of "harming state interests" and to "create a new person, a stable and spurious community, using the legitimacy enjoyed by the acts of public officials, launched a machinery detracting state funds in favor of one of its members, Lázaro Báez.

Regarding De Vido, Lopez, Carlos Kirchner and Periotti, having under its responsibility road activity and planning of public investment, he was accused of "having failed to control the activity of the units were under the purview of the ministry to office".

A Báez, who has six prosecutions and is imprisoned fifteen months, was accused of having made "an essential contribution" to the matrix of corruption investigated. First, for "having assembled and provided the necessary corporate structure to make it come together in the national state funds", as it was Austral Building (awarded 78.4% of road contracts).

Cristina Kirchner was prosecuted for illicit association and money laundering

Judge Claudio Bonadio, the cause Los Sauces SA, indicted former President, its Maximo and Florencia Kirchner sons and K, Lazaro Baez and Christopher Lee entrepreneurs "conspiracy in competition for money laundering and incompatible negotiations". He also seized Cristina Kirchner at 130 million pesos.

None of the accused may leave the country. The measure achieves the scribes involved in various operations. Judge also declared itself incompetent and suggested that the investigation into connectedness, continue in court presided by Judge Julian Ercolini who prosecuted Kirchner and Baez for conspiracy in the case investigating corruption in public works. The children of imprisoned businessman, were also processed.

The Kirchner family created Los Sauces SA in 2006

The estate was created in 2006 by Nestor, Cristina Kirchner and Max. Bonadio as its sole purpose was "the return or return" that "was done through leases owned by the company". And remarks that Los Sauces did not have a real seat, "has no employees working for the corporate purpose of the company, its employees, Angel Ramon Diaz Diaz (gardener ex Mandataria) and Florencia Kirchner that" you know what their tasks, as a board member or employee, or because a salary as an employee when it clearly does not perform work for society ".

For the first time the sons of former President are prosecuted in a corruption case, the judge described as "leaders of a band." Maximum Kirchner and Florence Kirchner have an embargo of $ 130 and $ 100 million respectively. For Báez the embargo was also $ 130 million, while the niece of former Mandataria -Romina Market-, it is an order of attachment of $ 100 million. Indalo Group owners, Christopher Lee and his partner Fabian De Sousa embargos were $ 100 million each. Osvaldo Sanfelice, deputy member of La Campora also was indicted and arrested. Indagas 21 people in the case, they ended processed.

Cristina Kirchner "head of a band," according to the judge Bonadio

In the case willows began with a complaint of Deputy Margarita Stolbizer (GEN) Bonadio considered that there is sufficient evidence to determine that Cristina and Maximo Kirchner are "ringleaders" which he joined after October 2010 "Florencia Kirchner having decision-making power in society". In this regard, he noted that the company never looked really be an estate but a network "personal and corporate to" perceive illegitimate money in order to give the appearance tender "and that the plan was concocted by" Nestor Carlos Kirchner, Cristina Elisabet Fernández, and Maximo Carlos Kirchner. "And Florence had a role" preponderant "after the death of his father.

Thus, according to the letter of over 200 pages, the judge found that after 21 investigations conducted, had "formed a band in order to receive money as payment for return of public works concession by lease agreements of signature "Los Sauces SA" Cristina Elisabet Fernández property, Maximo and Florencia Kirchner by companies called Báez Group, Indalo Group, Sanfelice Group, Creditworthiness SA and Mutual Association Forever Young ".

Cristina Kirchner and her children were processed by Bonadio.

Why he was processed Cristina Kirchner, his children and business partners ?. As "leaders of a band" and have "formed an organization that began to develop their criminal designs from May 2003 until the day December 14, 2016 day that judicial intervention is ordered" Los Sauces SA, "and the succession of Nestor Carlos Kirchner" in order to "receive money as illegitimate consideration for the granting of the concession of public works, of enabling gaming licenses and / or areas of the oil industry, and introduce it into the financial market , trying to give the appearance of lawful origin. "

Gils Carbo quote to read if he thought Alberto Nisman remove the AMIA prosecutor

The judge noted that the housing of the former president has earned for its operations of a corporate network formed companies Austral Group, Lázaro Báez (Kank y Costilla, Loscalzo and Del Curto, Austral Building, Valle Miter SA) and two companies of the Group Indalo: Inversora M & S and Alkalis of the Patagonia SA also noted that companies also participated Sanfelice, SA and Business Idea Patagónicos. This whole conglomeration of firms, were "benefiting large number of contracts with the National Government", while the two major shareholders of Los Sauces SA "They exercised the presidency of Argentina and executive and legislative positions in the province of Santa Cruz ".

Romina Mercado, daughter of Alicia Kirchner was also charged in Los Sauces SA. Photo Opi

Santa Cruz.

The judge declared himself incompetent and connectedness asked that the cause remains under investigation by the court by Julián Ercolini, who prosecuted for conspiracy to Cristina Kirchner and Baez, and a set of kirchnerista former officials.

The children of the owner of Austral Construcciones were also processed and embargos. In the case of Martin Báez by $ 20 million while his brothers Luciana and Leandro for $ 10 million each.

The cause Los Sauces SA began with a complaint of Deputy Margarita Stobilzer (GEN) in late 2015 after detecting a number of irregularities in the functioning of real estate and its main tenants were Christopher Lopez and Lazaro Baez.

Fraud will be judged by the State

Apart from other causes of corruption, the former president that Argentina government for two terms (2007-2015), Cristina Fernandez de Kirchner, who had succeeded in office by her husband Ernesto Kirchner, will sit on the accused bench prejudice the State motivated the so-called "dollar future," it happened after the crisis atmosphere where it was paid almost twice pesos per dollar than the official exchange.

Cristina wanted to face the real devaluation selling the so-called "dollar futures" ten pesos to be paid six months later.

Justice investigating this cause estimated at more than 3,500 million dollars prejudice to the measure to the Argentine state.

But the concern of the former president focuses on cases of corruption and illicit enrichment by those who should sit on the bench and jail time for her and for her family.

Remember that while Kirchner Argentina were ruling were amassing a billion-dollar fortune, according to witnesses, they weighed on scales as it was impossible to count the notes.

The Iranian threat attacks in Argentina Cristina Kirchner

It was at the Israeli embassy in March 1992 and 22 people being injured more than two hundred died. It was destroyed both the embassy and the consulate located in Buenos Aires Arrollo dalle.

Subsequently, two years later, another attack on the headquarters of the IMIA, the most important Jewish organization in Argentina mutual, where 85 people died. Those attacks were related to the shipment by the Argentine government two warships in 1991 to strengthen the US-led Gulf War against Iraq coalition.

Following investigations by US services Heznollah responsibility for the organization, supported by the Iranian state was established. And several Argentine authorities investigating the facts were found with high instances complicities that put in serious danger the same, so for many years did not work out.

It was the relationship of marriage Kirchner

with Venezuela, Cuba, Russia which were compromised if not hindered the investigation, so they decided to shelve and from the presidency to conclude the investigation, covering up the Iranian state, which basically was the responsible for these attacks.

The Nisman prosecutor, however, continued with investigations where senior Argentine government could be prosecuted and call the day before the president declare itself Cristina Fernandez found dead at his home in a shot. All indications are that the intelligence services were the authors as Nisman had revealed the cover-up of senior government officials, exjueces, exespías and some members of the Muslim community Argentina.

At present the investigation into the murder of prosecutor Nisman is unlikely to point out the responsibility of Cristina expresidenta and senior intelligence who organized crime.

Companies fear that Cristina

Kirchner will collapse and confess bribery

Companies that operated comfortably in Argentina Ernesto and Cristina Kirchner, including Telefonica, Claro and Telecom, fear that to avoid jail the former president confess everything he knows about the billions of dollars in bribes. At the same time, companies involved try to approach the government of President Macri for carpet corruption is not lifted, according to media knew mil21 Argentine intelligence.

Before the siege of Justice over allegations of illicit enrichment, Cristina Fernandez would be willing to reveal millionaires bribes which companies obtained favorable treatment by the Kirchner administration or charged unfair tariffs in the case of telecommunications companies.

During the nearly 13 years that both exercised as president of the nation Argentina-Ernesto (2003-2007) and Cristina (2007-2015) - they received thousands of millions of businesses. According to a report which has had accessmil21, Telefonica was pressured by Kirchner for alleged payment of one billion dollars to finance part of the electoral campaign in December 2007 that led Cristina Fernandez to the Casa Rosada, sedede the Presidency.

To avoid jail the former president would be willing to sue companies that offered bribes

Companies should not only regularly pay substantial "bites" but four election campaigns Kirchners defrayed by them. Leading multinational telecommunications allegedly involved in the extortion racket that allowed the enrichment of marriage and his inner circle were Claro (more than 20 million customers) Telecom Personal (18 million) and Telefónica (more than 16 million users) .

collaborators imprisoned

The former head of state is processed by a million-dollar plan for public works in the province of Santa Cruz, home of Kirchnerismo, which disappeared from the funds allocated to them. Federal Judge Julián Ercolini the accused in the car Cristina Fernandez as "criminally responsible coauthor of the crime of conspiracy in real competition with aggravated fraudulent administration for having committed against the public administration".

Fear of Cristina Fernandez to end up in jail is supported by the fact that his top aides have already entered prison. Jose Lopez, Secretary of Public Works, was arrested when he tried to hide 9 million in a convent in Buenos Aires. This character came to manage 9,000 million euros in infrastructure projects.

Ricardo Jaime, former Secretary of Transportation, is also in prison for corruption in buying useless to Spain and Portugal trains. Lázaro Báez, a bank teller in Santa Cruz when he met Ernesto Kirchner, became a billionaire businessman. It has also given their bones in prison.

Dozens of seized property

With the new government of Mauricio Macri Justice it is supported and carried out investigations that have begun by the seizure of dozens of properties, hotels and property of the former president. They are investigated to the assets of the couple's children, Max and Floren

Cristina Fernandez undergoes continuous depressive episodes forcing him to be medicated. It is under great emotional pressure and is almost deserted by all friends who in recent years joined his praetorian guard, according to information that has been coming mil21 access to intelligence means Argentina.

Companies try to negotiate with the Government Macri corruption carpet is lifted

Among his close it is said that if you guarantee judicial peace and does not enter prison, would be willing to betray Argentine and international companies that bribed members of the government for public works or expand their market shares without administrative setbacks in for telecommunications companies. They charged unfair tariffs no control. In exchange for enriching the leaders, they could boast a good income statement.

The Intelligence Secretariat (SI), the Argentine secret service, is monitoring unusual activity of companies trying to negotiate with the government of Mauricio Macri to the carpet of corruption that have been the saint for 13 years is not lifted and sign of Ernesto and Cristina Kirchner. Businesses, always according to these sources, would be offering all kinds of counterparts.

Telefonica investigates the alleged payment of one billion dollars to the Kirchners

President of Argentina, Mauricio Macri, has ordered the Justice and Intelligence Secretariat (SI) to investigate the alleged payment of one billion dollars by Telefonica to cover the 2007 election campaign that led Cristina Fernandez de Kirchner the Presidency of the nation. According to a report which has had access MIL21, the Spanish multinational was pressured by Kirchner to divert your bottom large sums of money for operations in Argentina smoothly. The former president is currently processed in several cases of corruption and illicit enrichment.

Buenos Aires is known to detail like marriage Kirchner, Nestor and Cristina, pressured corporations to finance the electoral campaign in December 2007. After eight years in power, Ernesto passed the baton to his wife, Cristina Fernandez, President of the Argentina nation.

The Ministry of Intelligence investigates Telefonica Argentina to which the Kirchners demanded one billion dollars as a donation for the 2007 election campaign

Apart from dark episodes, such as the suspicion that part of the campaign was financed with drug money, some of whose witnesses were killed the following year being sworn or briefcases from Venezuela, President Mauricio Macri has ordered to Justice and the Ministry of Intelligence (SI), the Argentine secret service, research the Spanish multinational Telefonica, which marriage demanded one billion dollars as a donation for this campaign, according to a documented report that has been MIL21 access.

Alierta trip to Buenos Aires

Apparently he had to intervene the president of Telefonica, Cesar Alierta, to negotiate the alleged bribery and what benefits they get in return the Spanish company, for which he traveled to Buenos Aires in one of the jet owned by Telefonica in December 2007 .

In Argentina abuse telephone companies like Claro and Movistar in application of opaque and unfair tariffs, which are beyond any control and where users are completely unprotected it is evident. Currently the expresidenta Cristina Fernandez has opened several fronts court convictions for corruption and money laundering in the 2007 election campaign.

In fact, already they have been processed by Ariel Lijo federal judge leading collectors of the presidential campaign of Cristina, accused of laundering funds called drug mafia. It is HéctorCapaccioli, Superintendent of Health Services and Sebastián Gramajo, who in that campaign was considered the official policymaker. Both have confessed that part of the campaign was financed with funds from drug trafficking.

Thousands of millions of large companies

Without the million-dollar contribution from large companies such as Claro and Telefonica campaign it would have been a disaster, so that justice, once out of Cristina Kirchner power, is willing to lift carpets and seek a declaration to those responsible for the companies involved with thousands of millions of dollars to finance election campaigns with the Kirchners and their circle of trust is enriched.

Some of the money moved in bags from the Casa Rosada, seat of the Presidency, to the cave (bank safe) that Kirchner made his mansion built in Calafate, in Patagonia.

Marriage accumulated dollars, euros and gold bullion in Calafate mansion for a golden retirement in Patagonia

Weighed tickets

When it was discovered that marriage accumulated an immense fortune in dollars, gold bullion and rare metals, witnesses processed declared that the Kirchners came to rack up as many tickets it was not possible to count and simply weigh them, to get a rough accounting of fortune which he was kept in the underground bobeda contruida purpose. Apparently they preferred to store money in five hundred euro banknotes because they occupied less space and weigh less than a hundred dollars. Some pointed to Telefónica as the company that provided them with these five hundred euro banknotes.

At present, apart from the alleged involvement of Telefonica in financing the election campaign of 2007, concern the president Macri is to recover the more than ten billion dollars have disappeared from public coffers and swelled the fortunes of the expresidenta Cristina Fernandez and dozens of senior positions during his tenure.

Cristina Kirchner prohibits receiving Juan Carlos at the airport, emeritus king waited four hours for you to pick the Spanish ambassador

The outgoing president of Argentina, Cristina Fernandez de Kirchner, expressly forbade his foreign minister that the king would receive emeritus upon arrival at Ezeiza airport in Buenos Aires. Juan Carlos and his entourage had to wait four hours until the Embassy of Spain provided them with transport. Some members of the delegation took taxis to the hotel they had booked. This incident adds to a series of arbitrary decisions Cristina Kirchner around the inauguration, on Thursday, December 10, the new president, Mauricio Macri.

Tantrums Cristina Fernandez de Kirchner

after losing the presidential election fill the Argentine news. The new president, Mauricio Macri, does not accept that the president will hand over the baton in Congress, as tradition demands that the transfer of power will take place in the Casa Rosada, seat of the Presidency, and the oath of office with earlier in Parliament to elected representatives.

This has caused a crisis among officials on the orders of the outgoing president, who have chosen to abandon their tasks among which were receiving foreign dignitaries attending the inauguration of Macri, held on Thursday, 10 December.

Cristina Kirchner ordered the foreign minister not to meet King acudiese emeritus, annoyed that Felipe VI has delegated its representation Juan Carlos

It was the case of King Juan Carlos of Bourbon

EmeritusWhich he landed at Ezeiza airport in Buenos Aires around seven pm on Tuesday, December 8 in an aircraft of the Spanish Air Force protocol without anyone Argentine government was to meet him. Major Stanislaus Ambassador settled into the room itself and airport authorities were making efforts phone until eleven at night. The old monarch and his bodyguards and officials traveling with the monarch, had to make do with cars embassy, having to use several taxis to move to the hotel they had booked.

Was the Foreign Minister, Hector Timerman, in charge of protocol, who received taxativas orders of President Fernandez de Kirchner not to go out to meet Juan Carlos, annoyed that although he had officially invited to King Philip VI of Bourbon, he has delegated his father, who retired in Argentina consider the Royal House.

As outgoing president has not gotten the oath of office the new president in a solemn ceremony in parliament, would become a tribute to the greater glory of Cristina, it has forbidden the 150 deputies and senators Justicialismo, his party, They are attending the swearing Macri in Parliament.

The delivery of the baton will be held later in the Casa Rosada thanks to Judge Maria Servini de Cubria set for midnight on 9 December, the end of the mandate of Cristina Kirchner, so she no longer will decide where will celebrate the event.

Nor will hand the baton

But there's more. Breaking the most basic democratic norms and respect for the decision of the Argentine people expressed at the polls, the outgoing president has announced that it will not deliver him to Mauricio Macri neither staff, nor the band, because he did not attend the ceremony.

According to the official, at 11:15 local time on Thursday, December 10, Macri reach the National Congress escorted by the Mounted Grenadiers Regiment. At 12 noon swearing-in ceremony before the Legislature and then deliver a speech that will start the presidential term begins.

After the ceremony, Macri and his wife will move to the Government House where at 13:30 hours the act of transfer of control attributes in the White Room before authorities of the Nation and foreign leaders will be held, including the king emeritus Juan Carlos, who as been published MIL21 insists that he take charge Zarzuela missions representing the Spanish monarchy.

It is ordered silence the Argentine shameful episode

Since Zarzuela it comes to mitigate as much as possible the impact of the incident, trying to silence with conflicting information, denying that Juan Carlos took a taxi at the airport Ezezia, when the reality is that it was not received as befits an authority representing the State Spanish, although his condition has angered king emeritus outgoing president, Cristina Fernandez de Kirchner.

However the Argentina press has echoed the formal disaster organized by the abandonment of its obligations under the government of Cristina Fernandez de Kirchner. Eight presidents and 42 foreign delegations met with an awkward situation to reach Argentina. In fact, the new president, Macri, ordered to try to organize the presence of dignitaries and making a hole in his difficult day, received before the oath to King Juan Carlos, who apologized on behalf of Argentina for failing It has been treated as he deserved his arrival in Buenos Aires.

Campaigns financed by drug money

Cristina Kirchner covers and grabbed headlines when the news that a victim of a triple homicide, who was related to drug trafficking, had helped finance the election campaign of the president.

It all started with a triple murder scandal that shocked the country and appeared on every cover: three young entrepreneurs disappeared one week; when their bodies were found, they did so lifeless and injuries that showed they had been tortured before his death. The three men: Sebastian Forza, Damian Ferron and Ariel Vilán. The first two were engaged in the business of medicines; Vilan, advertising. But the fact that hit squarely on the government of Kirchner was that he had received from the victims of homicide generous checks, which served for the President would make a blind eye to the illegal trade and the export and import of ephedrine, main chemical needed to synthesize methamphetamine. In this point,

After the spark has been ignited as to who were the patrons of the campaign of Argentina, the case began to unravel when several businessmen claimed to have figured in the list of "donors" funds for the campaign of Kirchner in the record he came to power by judge Maria Servini de Cubria. However, entrepreneurs, among whom was present Gabriel Brito, declared that even though their names were on the payroll of the President, the reality was that it did not contribute capital to its cause.

But there was evidence that someone helped finance the 2007 election campaign, and after lengthy investigations by the judge in 2008 came to light, thanks to a report from the US Embassy in Buenos Aires that part of that funding came from the FARC, particularly drug trafficking. Upon learning this information, investigators in the case considered then they'd just solve another mystery knew therefore the source of the $ 800,000 that had been intercepted in 2007 at the Customs Ezeiza Airport in Buenos Aires, package arrived on a private flight from Caracas; if there was a drug cartel collaborating with the expenses of the campaign, it was concluded that other patrons might be those belonging to the Mexican Sinaloa cartel.

The Argentine government corruption is an issue deservedly popular does not mean that necessary legislature after legislature; however, it is logical that reconstruction and sanitation public sector is and will be viable provided the government does not act against the lawlessness in all sectors, from drug traffickers to corrupt businessmen. With symbiotic relationships between governments and corrupt businessmen, political security in Argentina will be a utopia and will repeat the pattern that has been taking place in the South American country for years.

Brito raises his voice

Businessman Gabriel Brito, who was mixed into the murky issue of drug trafficking, reacted by denouncing the Kirchner-Fernández for illicit enrichment, as he was involved in the Kirchner spiral without knowing it: he declared in 1997, was Nestor Lorenzo, a friend of Brito and owner of the drugstore San Javier, who asked him a blank check to help with a bad financial situation. Brito did not care, trusted him, so he did not ask or investigate the operation. However, "after two months', he declared the newspaper Profile-, FIU officials questioned me about who had donated 310,000 pesos to FPV (Front for Victory party, Kirchner). I told them I had never contributed anything to the party. They showed me a photocopy of checks ... It was then that I opened my eyes ".

Contributions from drug traffickers and mafias

Argentina's deputy Elisa Carrió, leader of the Civic Coalition, denounced the rumor that Argentina's President Cristina Fernandez de Kirchner received drug traffickers and mafias checks to finance his election campaign.

"It is imperative that Judge Lijo active once the criminal case and investigate Gabriel Brito, Nestor Lorenzo, and other contributors to the campaign of Cristina Kirchner because today all those involved in the drug mafia who are detained or who are dead were contributed money to the campaign of 2007, "said several deputies of the Civic Coalition.

The leader of the complaint said former campaign manager Fernandez de Kirchner, the administrator of Health, Hector Capaccioli as the protagonist of the "way of funding" electoral. "The way of funding clearly comes to (former chief of staff) Alberto Fernandez and Capaccioli" said the former presidential candidate. "Relationships are explicit, and if now Alberto Fernández has some relationship with Cristina, you conclude," suggested Carrio.

The triple murder related to trafficking in ephedrine manufacture of drugs, drug traffickers Sebastián Forza (34 years), Damian Ferron (37) and Leopoldo Bina (35) in General Rodriguez, could be the straw that broke the camel of rumors that had been giving since the beginning of the electoral campaign of Kirchner and which has sparked all these statements of the opposition. Shortly after the news of the murder was confirmed that one of the victims contributed money to the 2007 campaign of Cristina.

The investigation reached this point when the terrible suicide of the owner of a drugstore Ariel Vilan, who maintained relations with Forza met. Between the two they could have contributed to the campaign of Cristina $ 100,000 in six checks. While all this is denied by every one of those involved in the campaign, the tests do see that contributions from drug traffickers to the electoral campaign were true.

Even Gabriel Brito, one of those accused of being part of a conspiracy in the case of adulterated drugs, confessed to having contributed more than $ 300,000 in checks to the campaign of Cristina unbeknownst to him. Among his statements he said, "I found that they ended up there after the triple crime". "If I have to pay something to justice I will pay, but I have not participated in any drug adulteration maneuver". For all these statements Brito has been released due to lack of evidence regarding the crimes of extortion and money laundering.

Everyone involved in the plot:

Torres, Carlos Luciano contributed $ 170,000 and was arrested because drug mafia. Torresin, Carlos Horacio are the same person (Torres Carlos Luciano) $ 155,000. Total contributed by these two names that correspond to the same person, $ 325,000.

Multipharma SA contributed $ 310,000. Holders of the company are Nestor Lorenzo and Carlos Torres, who in turn brought a second contribution of $ 66,000. Lorenzo was arrested because drug mafia and suspected of links with the triple crime and trafficking in ephedrine. Total contributed by Multipharma, Lorenzo Torres: 376,000 dollars.

Global Pharmacy SA contributed $ 310,000. The owner is Gabriel Brito and was arrested because of drug mafia.

Droguería Urbana SA contributed $ 310,000. The owner is Daniel Hendler and maintained relations with Forza and Ariel Vilan, who financed one of its pharmacies. Audifarm SA contributed $ 140,000, brought in 2006 by Daniel Hendler.

SEACAMP SA contributed $ 200,000 and the owner Sebastián Forza was killed in triple murder of General Rodriguez.

Droguería Unifarma SA contributed $ 160,000 and the owner Martin Magallanes and Vilan Ariel Damian Ferron was also killed General Rodriguez Triple Crime and was a pharmacist trader.

Leopoldo Bina, also assassinated, General Rodriguez Triple Crime

Ariel Vilan committed suicide by jumping from his parents' apartment where he was hiding from the investigation. Uniforma worked at the drugstore, investigated by the drug mafia, whose owner was Martin Magallanes.

Marcos Emiliano also committed suicide when he was hit by a train on 15 November 2009. Their leader was Pablo Quaranta who was a company Ibar Pérez Corradi, drugstore Odin Concep SRL. Another partner of Odin Concept SRL is Jorge Adrian Cabrera, who in turn is a partner of Martin Lanatta in Elvesta Argentina SA, arrested and charged with the triple murder.

Ibar Perez Lorenzo Corradi partner of course, had trade links with Forza, allegedly threatened by a debt of money. He is currently detained to be extradited to the US for trafficking in oxycodone. Linked to the cause of drug mafia and trafficking in ephedrine.

Cristina lovers

The Kirchners were a couple of power. Love ends when he left as governor in Santa Cruz and she starts living in Buenos Aires, in the best corner of the city. Both have had lovers, but their political project forced them to stay together, "says La Razon, Sylvina Walger, author of" Cristina, the whole truth about the president.

"The Cessna Citation governorate flying from Rio Gallegos to Buenos Aires. On board were Kirchner, Cristina and the deputy governor of the province, Chiquito Arnold. 1995 ran and then marriage was traveling frequently to the capital to visit the Menem's economy minister, Domingo Cavallo, a friend and ally. Midair, Kirchner read something that did not like the "La pavada" section of the Chronicle newspaper: they spoke of an ostentatious choker $ 30,000, according to the publication, sported his wife, the flamboyant candidate for national senator. Governor furious. And before Arnold, he raised his arm and hit

Cristina with daily head.

'I told you those things do not ever put the!

Cristina also turned red:

'But what you do! Have you gone crazy?

I was so furious as he. But there was a witness and not managed to answer the coup. Were all three together on a plane and could not throw Arnold with a parachute through the door to settle the matter privately.

During the rest of the flight, none spoke again. The tension was unbearable. Chronicle copy was left undone.

When Kirchner argued and began to raise his voice, marriage collaborators knew that it was time to retreat. The they left alone. But aboard the Cessna Citation was no way.

I never saw anything like it recalled years later Arnold. He stuck with the newspaper, like a dog. "

This is just one case of these fights but lovers of the Peronist widow romances have been aired by various anti-Kirchner media. For example what infers the magazine "News" and dare not say directly, is what within the ruling party keep quiet or silent all: her love affair with Vice President Amado Boudo (51 years).

"It's a secretvoicesIt is known not only in the

Government House, but also in certain ministries and departments. Those who know what Callan, usually by embarrassment, by the latent memory of the recent death of Nestor Kirchner ", say from this publication.

CFK lovers: Boudou

The best kept secret of Cristina Fernandez de Kirchner are freckles. Few have seen them because the president is careful to appear in full view of everyone. His black suits makeup widow and generous help in the effort to camouflage them. Moles Cristina Fernandez could be a perfect metaphor for what hides the president Argentina. And what are the mysteries that hides the lady is? Lindner Franco, an Argentine journalist who has just published 'lovers Cristina' (Planeta), describes the widow of Nestor Kirchner as "the woman who surrounds himself with ambitious young officers and often straight out of a casting of models."

Cristina Fernandez (60 years) has always had a reputation for "assails cots" because lovers preferred much younger than her. Pintureros boys that the author of the book refers are, among others, Amado Boudou (51 years), current vice president of the country.

One year after taking the reins of Argentina, Cristina Boudou who commissioned by the Ministry of Economy was made. And that her husband Nestor Kirchner did not make him any grace this dapper man, who was nicknamed 'the Frenchman'.

The book's author argues that Boudou, a crazy motorcycles and electronic music, have dazzled Cristina Fernandez from virtually the day she met him, and when the couple had a discussion about Boudou, Fernandez will endilgó husband " what happens is you're jealous. "

In fact there is a picture he took a businessman in September 2009 throughout Argentina nobody has dared to publish. In the snapshot shows how Fernández leans her head on the shoulder of his protégé and looks at him with rapture.

Currently it is not known whether Boudou remains on the list of the president's affections. You may have changed his mind after the intelligence service of the country recorded a phrase that makes very bad place to number two in the government: "How ugly is Cristina without makeup," said her lover, whose indiscretion surely cost face.

And, as argued in the book, the sin of Boudou would be to be too familiar. Apparently, in conversation he called Fernandez de Kirchner as 'mom', which unfortunately for Boudou, also reached the ears of the aforementioned.

"-Do not worry. Today I talk with mommy and you fix the problem.

Amado Boudou gave the phrase a conspiratorial tone perfectly found his friend on the other side of the line. "The Mummy" was none other than

Cristina Fernandez de Kirchner, the widow and reelected President a few days before with 54 percent of the vote. And the friend who listened to Boudou and pretended festejarle his nonchalance was Jorge Brito, Kirchner banker, ex menemista and Macro owner, the financial institution sector the Government had blamed for the exchange run that followed the triumph of Cristina at the polls.

Brito did the first thing he could think of at the time: he called his friend Boudou to defend themselves.

'I're killing he told the vice-president brand. You know that I have nothing to do ...

And that's when his friend uttered the phrase confianzuda:

-Today same talk with mommy and you fix the problem.

How serious the matter is that the President found out. It was not a rumor, nor any witnesses, but because they heard the recording of the telephone conversation between the vice president and the banker. Four sources affirm government, including an official who is a friend of Boudou, a leader of La Campora and a collaborator of the Ministry of Intelligence.

The official who is a friend of Boudou sums up what certainly give him and his government colleagues:

I know that Aimé was disgraced by desubicados comments made by phone.

Aimé Boudou is what they call their friends is the French translation of his name, Amado.

How he did the recording at the hands of the President? The sources agree: Hector was first Icazuriaga, the head of government spies who approached him that evidence Maximo Kirchner, the president's son. Icazuriaga and Maximum are inseparable: each time the head of La Campora puts someone in his sights, Secretary of Intelligence collects unofficial information that the young Kirchner requested, as before the requested his late father. "

Wednesday November 30, 2011, two weeks after the phone slip, the President surprised everyone when he publicly chastised who until then was his favorite.

Well, now we go with the conchetos of Puerto Madero 'I gave the floor to Boudou in a video conference that it was inaugurating an industrial park in the locality of Berazategui, and him in the most expensive neighborhood in the capital.

Boudou, annoyed, took off a giggle and was encouraged to respond:

-Not only for conchetos of Puerto Madero, as you said, but Puerto Madero has become a cakewalk for thousands of locals that come here on weekends Coast Highway ... ".

The troubled past of this Don Juan

Volume, juicy anecdotes palatial recreates the childhood of "Aimé"He pronounced Eme, and so nicknamed him Boudou in his íntimo- in Mar del Plata environment; Step five schools; stumbles in rugby; youth nights in clubs like Happy Sobremonte and Maria Lopez; talent as a disc jockey; and conflicting nightclub

"How was I to know 'Aimé' in that place where mounted a nightclub back in the late eighties had worked on the dictatorship a center of clandestine detention?" A close friend of Boudou who attended the inauguration asks the disco, in late 1989.

And that is addicted to music, the young Boudou refitted an old aristocratic house of colonial style, which had failed to work in any area, and set up a nightclub two stories which he called Pop Art, who years later would be renamed Villajoyosa. It was located on the side of Route 11, in the suburbs of Mar del Plata, in the Camet Park, where the sea air is suffering much more than in the center of Mar del Plata.

The dance floor in the main hall, was in the middle of a pool dotted with palm trees, where ever a young man fell excess alcohol. Among the hallways a foul odor seeping, from sewage plant, located meters away.

Boudou was a kind of owner, public relations and said he was receiving guests and passed the music. It was the visible face of a club that came to survive only four months.

Not only because it was away from the

traditional area of nightclubs, on Constitution Avenue, but because its interior intricate and "something" that something was flying over the environment "who came to discover with the passing of the years did not invite young people to shop around the site.

¿Amores summer or searches of power?

In those years, he had begun a youthful romance with Cecilia Venturino, one of four daughters of "Chiquito" Venturino, the master of the garbage business in Mar del Plata.

This donjuán all swore loyalty to them, but in fact was not one of his greatest virtues. His fleeting summer romances were the delight among his friends, who alternated between rugby adolescence and nights in the disco Maria Lopez.

A couple of years later, and for a long time, the affair most remembered derisively by his friends was the relationship during a summer "Aimé" shared Barbara Bengolea granddaughter businesswoman Fortabat and daughter Ines Lafuente after learning by chance a mid January 80

Bengolea was a young somewhat overweight, but Boudou gave no importance. Quite the contrary: among his friends laughed. What a "Aimé" really attracted him was that Bengolea driving a yellow Volkswagen Gol emerging in the automotive market and moving through Mar del

Plata accompanied by bodyguards young. "What attracted her power," recalls a friend. In your group, Amado bragged and bragged their relationship with the car. The romance lasted only one summer: Family Bengolea advised him away from that young man because it was not good influence.

And its fleeting and not as romances are many others: Marina Mendiguren -sobrina of José Ignacio, president of the Industrial Union Argentina and who Boudou, to date, greets under the nickname Uncle and Agustina Seguin are other dazzled to reach his current partner, journalist Agustina Kampfer, who wowed during an interview and clouded on the first date, when he happened to look in his Harley Davidson.

All for power

In choosing the last week of August 1987 for the Student of the Faculty of Economics and Social Sciences of the National University of Mar del Plata, Boudou is presumed to have slept with two students stripped of conventional aesthetics still they would not have defined their vote. At least, that is what they say a dozen colleagues, friends and teachers who enthusiastically recall this anecdote.

Some of them still scandalized: he slept with the two fat to convince them that vote !, relates the anecdote involving the now Vice-president and former economy minister, she says journalist

Federico Mayol in his book Amado . The true story of Boudou.

Through interviews, Mayol, author of this entire book devoted to this unique political, details how in youth, Boudou in enlisted in the ranks of the UCeDe (more to attract women because he was interested in politics, holds) and embraced neoliberalism; his admiration for former President Carlos Menem, privatization and the Convertibility; and contempt for Peronism, although he understood, and he confessed to his friends, who was the only way to climb in Argentina politics.

Also it tells the behind the scenes of his days in the civil service and its first steps in front of the Ministry of Economy: building a small adjoining gym to his office and the purchase of 19 high-end automobiles kilometer zero for the Palace Finance; its relationship with the number one Banco Macro, Jorge Brito (former "banker Nestor) and the close link ensued, during the campaign, with Hebe de Bonafini and then seized the Foundation mothers of Plaza de Mayo, Sergio Schoklender.

Seconds beforeannounceAmado Boudou was chosen to accompany her, to the chagrin of another of his alleged lovers, Cristina Kirchner stressed his loyalty and courage and ranked these attributes as fundamental to face the coming times. Also before saying his name, he recalled that Boudou was the one who brought the idea of nationalizing pensions in mid 2008. But he did as a minister but as head of the Anses, where would directly by election of the current President.

A snake charmer

Young promise as a DJ and inveterate liberal head of the Anses, economy minister (a position he assumed in July 2009) and Vice President of the Nation in the ranks of the Front for Victory.

An upstroke that had mentors and Sergio Massa, current mayor of Tigre, Benigno Vélez, former General Manager of the Central Bank, but would have enjoyed the confidence of Alberto Fernandez and Alicia Kirchner, when Nestor Kirchner was still alive, details Mayol. "

The most surprising is how a guy who always lived without limits, cheeky, seductive, intelligent, was seducing each of the people who went across in his political career since he arrived in Mar del Plata, at the end of 1992 to today, and how very few merits became vice president of a day to the other, analyzes Mayol.

In this regard, the journalist says were those weapons of seduction which used also to have the approval of the President. He seduced her from the first moment, since they met in May 2008, before she appointed him as head of the Anses.

Boudou used that seduction to lure. There is a

former official who defines the relationship with Cristina as a political unromance says. The book brings to mind another story: "Today I met a divine boy, is perfect to put in front of the Anses, tells Mayol that Cristina had confessed to them while they dined at Olives, Kirchner and Alberto Fernandez, then chief of staff, who was quick to respond: Cristina, that guy will bring you problems, we engage in some weird things. You two are jealous, I will designate and ready, would have ended the conversation the first president.

Boudou was always more Cristinista that Kirchnerista.

Boudou replaced Carlos Fernandez as head of the Economy Ministry on July 8, 2009. He was part of Cristina Kirchner decided replacement for (and Nestor, of course) cimbronazo after the heavy defeat in the legislative elections days earlier.

At the same ceremony, Aníbal Fernández replaced Sergio Massa in the Cabinet and Julio Alak occupied the vacancy left the first in the Ministry of Justice.

But it soon became clear that Boudou would be relegated to the same background than their predecessors in Economics from the exit of Roberto Lavagna government. Kirchner was still the boss of the economy.

Idyll away now living with the President, his relationship with Kirchner had several stormy passages.

Luxury cars: the federal justice still investigating Boudou for the purchase of 19 high-end vehicles without public bidding, in December 2009, five months after taking over as minister. The cars were purchased from the company Guido Guidi SA for $ 2,301,227.25 to "meet operational needs" of the Ministry of Economy. Besides Boudou, they are charged with the legal and administrative secretary of the ministry, Benigno Vélez.

The crisis of reservations: although he had a minor role in the conflict with Martin Redrado, who starred slip angered Kirchner. It was the young marplatense who, as President of the Central Bank already had one foot out (but had not yet resigned), he said that his replacement would be Mario Blejer, the head of the Central Bank during the government of Duhalde, while Buenos Aires was boiling between heat and reservations fight was in France, first accepted, but few hours later backtracked.

He rejected the offer of Boudou when he

learned that not only Redrado had not resigned, but neither the executive had the power to remove him from office.

And then they ran hard rumors that Kirchner thought him off, but the blood did not reach the river since then Boudou was part of the group of ministers disempowered no room for maneuver.

It was an open secret that Kirchner made the decisions concerning the economy (especially inflation) alone, and when asked his advice did Guillermo Moreno and even his former finance ministers, but never Boudou.

Negotiations with the IMF: in August 2010, Kirchner moved to Boudou negotiating with the IMF. He appointed as Argentine delegate to the Alfredo Mac Laughlin fund, an official at its narrowest confidence.

Photo with Favale: on October 24, 2010, three days before the death of Kirchner, transcended the photos that appeared Amado Boudou embraced Cristian Favale, the main accused (today accused) for the murder of Mariano Ferreyra.

The images were taken during a meeting of the Epoka, the rock that Boudou then organized every Wednesday to honor other kirchneristas in the tearoom La Puerto Rico.

The crime of militant young PO very concerned Kirchner, while those who were close to him during those days say was obsessed with his resolution.

In addition, the dissemination of photos of Boudou with barrabrava accused of having killed Ferreyra coincided with the government's attempt to link Eduardo Duhalde with José Pedraza Using photos of a meeting between the two who had more than one year old.

With Schoklender: In February 2011, Boudou accompanied Schoklender in housing delivery of the Mothers of Plaza de Mayo Foundation in the Club Albariños. The relationship with former agent of the company was buried and tried minimized when the scandal broke. Pictured Boudou runs the resort with Hebe de Bonafini and then right hand.

It was not the only time the Minister shared the stage with Schoklender. On 24 March last, the new candidate for vice participated in the Central Market in an event organized by the Mothers. In those days, Boudou was still a candidate for the head of city government and Bonafini was one of the mainstays of his campaign.

That day also were the Secretary of Domestic Trade and also brand new candidate for vice, but Daniel Scioli, the head of the Federal Authority of Audiovisual Communication Services (AFSCA), Gabriel Mariotto. Bonafini closed the list of speakers and ceremony

Chosen by love

In 2009, a year after taking his first presidential term, Cristina put in front of the Ministry of Economy despite the objections of her husband Nestor Kirchner, who doubted the suitability of the "Frenchie" fond of electronic music and Motorcycle high end. Kirchner assumed, with confidence, that the prettyboy economist had seduced his wife with youthful impudence of his 45 years. "What happens is you're jealous," he said the president, giving settle the matter, as it did previously when he chose for ANSE.

Two years later, the inhabitants of River View, a building located in the exclusive neighborhood of Puerto Madero, found that the property had been invaded by a contingent of taciturn boys who insisted, unsuccessfully, to go unnoticed. "They were not the usual custodians of Amado Boudou. These other belonged to the safety device of the president. The neighbors wonder what would Cristina at that time, in the apartment of the minister," said Sandra, a resident, the author of the book Cristina lovers.

And the head of the government relied increasingly on his economy minister, not only in the figurative sense of the word. In September 2009, one of the businessmen attending the ceremony lending to SMEs in the Casa Rosada took a picture in the host appeared with his head resting on the shoulder of Boudou. "He seemed relaxed and oblivious to what was happening around him. Out of respect for the president I did not show anyone the picture," said the entrepreneur Franco Lindner.

Why she chose him as vice Cristina?

He chose for confidence. Boudou put it in a pocket entry Cristina when he met her. He was pleased with the figure of Boudou. Several officials speak of "political affair". Politically, Cristina fell in love with Boudou. In fact, when Nestor dies, she relies heavily on Boudou. Nestor Kirchner alive Vice President Boudou would have been unthinkable. In fact, he was struck in the kirchnerismo appointment. Throughout his political and non-political career, Boudou was falling well with everyone has that ability and that seduction. It is their main political weapon.

But probably, at this time Cristina Kirchner this good regretted having appointed Aimé, as his friends call him, as his number two for the elections of September 23, 2011. Shortly after Boudou took office as vice president, Service State Intelligence (SIDE) recorded a conversation he had with a group of close, which proclaimed, quote: "What is Cristina ugly without makeup."

The video came at the hands of Máximo Kirchner who burst into a rage at her mother's office. "How can you allow that guitarist basuree you," exclaimed before the astonished gaze of the president and one of his advisers, present there. It was too late to remove from office who had nailed him a dagger into the depths of her feminine pride. But since then, says the author, Cristina Kirchner never again lay his head on the shoulder of Amado Boudou.

However after the incident Ciccone, with allegations of corruption and conspiracy, managed to lose sleep and Vice end their possible political aspirations to replace the President. "

Before he was happy, Boudou repeated in an intimate setting. Ciccone did not sit well in your circle. Boudou was a candidate to succeed Cristina in 2015. Now he is not comfortable with this position. I had to get out of your routine. You can not go eat at places that were regular. His political career is finished. No days beyond the Kirchners.

Axel Kicillof, the lover I expropriate YPF

At a meeting of alumni of Colegio Nacional Buenos Aires, in which they talked about football, music and 'mine' (women) someone turned the conversation to Cristina Kirchner. It was at that moment thatAxel Kicillof (42 years) boasted of having "Hypnotized" the president. Many have thought that boasted of his reputation heartbreaker, but his closest friends knew economist 40 years ever insinuate such a thing. And the spell that says exercise concernsCristina's admiration for his intellectual gifts and the boldness of his ideas. Suffice it to say that it was Axel who led her to think aboutexpropriation of YPF, Output of the energy crisis affecting the country.

At the Casa Rosada also attributed the authorship of 'Public Utility Project'; the expropriation document circulated last Thursday between government MPs and stood war the Spanish government and the European Union.

Threats from the old continent Cristina forced to rethink the strategy of going for all it had taken. But if anyone thought Kicillof would be disgraced for not having foreseen the consequences that would bring the plan arrodillar the Spanish partners YPF, is because it ignores one of the most pronounced features of Cristina: his unswerving loyalty to the people who earn their affected. President leaves injured on the battlefield."Most likely it is that Axel continue to visit the presidential office when he pleases and Cristina leave everything aside to listen to their proposals"A Kirchner administration official told reporters.

This is the official version of events, but there are others that suggest that the decision to snatch Repsol YPF emerged otherwise.

All indications are that after nationalization of YPF (Argentina subsidiary of Repsol) urdida between cap and cap for the alleged lover Cristina Fernandez de Kirchner, Axel KicillofThe company will maximum speed for oil exploration to the Government of Spain has given its approval.

Get ready for a real battle in the Canaries, as activity in the vicinity of the islands of Fuerteventura and Lanzarote could start right away. Repsol is a company, which more than anything, he understands only your bottom line; and lack of bread (Argentina), are good cakes (Canary Islands). While there is little agreement with the ways that has been given carte blanche Repsol to search for oil in the Canaries, it may be good, facing international markets, which expropriate Repsol, as things stand Argentina's battered situation.

WhileErnesto Kirchner(Deceased husband of Cristina Fernandez) privatized YPF, Argentina could not attend because withdrawals, is now his widow of emulativeEva Duarte de Peronwhich plunders. Should at least change its name battle, which is that of Cristina Kirchner, on the oneCristina KicillofWhich is the name of the young deputy minister of economy nights glad the president alcove dishonoring her husband (for their actions no alcove, but politicians) and put at the feet of the horses to their country.

A brilliant young man

Looks younger than it has and the position held Vice Minister of Economy- has not influenced her simple dress or direct way it is expressed. According to the newspaper Clarin, at the last meeting that he and Planning Minister held with Antonio BrufauAxel demanded the Spanish executive"Return" 15,000 million dollars Repsol "has been" in Argentina in recent years.

Kirchnerista rivals in court say the president admiration for his intellectual gifts makes him feel superior to other ministers. But actuallythe aura of the thinker was not given the president but Máximo Kirchner, who maintains a close friendship Axel. He was the eldest son of Cristina who invited him to join the Campora is the youth group of the Kirchners. "The fact that Kicillof graduated with honors from the University of Buenos Aires and in his student founded a" think tank "dedicated to the analysis of the theories of Marx and John Keynes, made a deep impression on Max and then his mother, "says Lucas Parson, a former militant of La Campora. The movement is said to Axel scholarship he inherited his great-grandfather, a famous rabbi of Odessa (Russia) and their parents, a psychoanalyst connoted and a psychologist.

In early 2009, Maximo Kirchner encouraged his friend to move from theoretical to action. The first charge was obtained fromfinancial manager of Aerolineas Argentinas, A company that since its nationalization in 2008 continues to produce losses. The red numbers of the company did not prevent the brain from K Administration continue climbing positions to be admitted to the exclusive club that manages the country's economy, where the holder of that portfolio, Hernán Lorenzino, is the least influencing decisions they are taken. In that forum, Guillermo Moreno has the role of enforcer of harsh government policies, such as the imposition of import barriers and forcing producers to keep prices frozen. Planning Minister Julio De Vido with his vast experience and moderation, represents the kind face of the troika. YAxel Kicillof provides fuel to keep alive the flame ideological which can cause fire as he was about to consume the links between Argentina and Spain.

VanityFair also includes this controversy

Not Brad Pitt. Nor Ricky Martin. The Spanish version of the magazine*Vanity Fair*has echoed also the rising fame of Argentine Economy Vice Minister,Axel Kicillof, So he published an intimate biography with pictures of his family and his private life secrets left bare his personality to rise within the Argentine government.

The famous magazine that Kicillof, 41 years old, married, father of two children but presumed to have"Hypnotized Cristina". The publication calls him"gallant"and "one of thebrains of the Argentine expropriation of YPF ".

IsMaximum close friend, The eldest son of Néstor Kirchner and Cristina Fernandez de Kirchner

Its link with Kirchner does not end at Maximus. At an informal meeting declared (without mincing words):"A Cristina I have hypnotized"

As reported in the Argentine newspaper La Nacion, Kiciloffgo three or four times a week at the Casa Rosadaand crosses the residence of the president as if anduviese for his own home. "Cristina is delighted with Axel," admitted that Article

In the corridors of the Casa Rosada many define it as one of the ministers whomore accessHe is the president and as Boudou has also been in charge of the economy, we do not know if more or less success.

But to choose their top aides, or appoint officials significance, rigor is not applied precisely what the Chief Argentina- says the author of "Los Amantes de Cristina". She alone is enough that impress. On April 17, 2012, the economist Axel Kicillof corresponded to defend the expropriation of oil company YPF before the Senate. According to the story of Franco Lindner, after branded as "parsley", "parrots", "morons" and "guitar free market" to those present, she declared: "I love that guy yes it is politically incorrect.".

Now he swaggers with the pompous title of Secretary for Economic Policy and Development Planning, which is incomprehensible to his detractors that minimize their flight as an economist. If you are in power it is because encadila Fernandez.

Lindner explains: "What Kicillof has on its rivals is something like what happens to the male audience with the heartthrobs of Hollywood like Brad Pitt, adored by women Its air prodigy, smarty child and above prettyboy makes. feel threatened. (...)

His friends from Colegio Nacional de Buenos Aires, who did not try to Axel, or Alec, but Ax, remember what I told them Kicillof days after taking office in the Ministry of Economy. (...) 'And how do you get on with it?', They asked. 'The'm hypnotized' Ax said. And everyone laughed. "

Had he been alive Nestor Kirchner, probably could have spoken Kicillof so strong he meant. Fernandez Kirchner was possessive and vice versa.

... "Cristina and Nestor is celaban him to her, and she him (...) once asked her what she would do in case of an infidelity of her husband replied: 'If I cheat, I first kill. And then divorce me, "recounts Lindner.

Kirchner's former collaborators remember the day that would have taken the flaps to a custodian of the President, Diego Carbone, to shout: 'You turn away near her and I'll kill you!'. Kirchner thought he detected some approximation of the custodian to Cristina and acted accordingly. "

Other loves and veiled hints:

'Cristina lovers' (Planeta), describes the widow of Nestor Kirchner as "the woman who surrounds himself with ambitious young officers and often straight out of a casting of models." The book's title promises more than it actually provides, as the author also attributed a string of lovers to the president. Lindler shown often very winding and suggests more things that affirms all of the law, as we reflect below.

The trio Storani, Cristina and a friend

Lindner also in his book that the former Radical deputy Federico Storani received a bold proposal by a mutual friend with Cristina Kirchner. Storani ensures that declined the invitation and could never really see if Argentina President today would have participated in that meeting.

"- What if we add to Cristina - had asked her friend and friend Cristina who thought they could have fun all three together.

Storani not know what to do. After an interminable silence, he struck him a flash of lucidity. Answered:

-No better not. It is for quilombo.

The friend made him increasingly bold proposals, but this time had gone too far. Include the then deputy Cristina Fernandez de Kirchner at a tripartite meeting?

Two respectable Deputies and a friend in common, the blonde and sexy lawyer from La Plata to which Storani had met in the summer of 1998, and Cristina frequented since his days of youth in the 70s in the provincial capital.

- Really you do not want, Fredi? she insisted.

-Better not sniffed it.

UCR deputy interior minister and future of the Alliance intuited that was a bad idea. Her friend used to chase in vain with bold offers, he proposed games, triangles and high voltage fantasies, but never before had told her about Cristina. Storani was his colleague in the House and had only exchanged a few words. It seemed an attractive woman. But he was not willing to risk his reputation and his family.

These things know how to begin but not how they end -desalentó her friend.

Cristina's friend, despite his insistence, had not achieved the deputy yielded to the temptation of his increasingly daring proposals. Storani liked her, but the provocative flirtation was never consummated because he refused knighthood modes. He would never have allowed a slip. The only time he was wondering was when she offered:

'And if we add to Cristina? ".

Miriam Quiroga and Miguel Nunez, lovers

After being cast by Cristina, Miriam Quiroga, identified as one of the oldest lovers of former President Nestor Kirchner, working on writing a book that tells the story of his relationship with the former president. In these pages recounts, among other things, a fight he had with Kirchner in which he tells his wife, Cristina, and then spokesman Miguel Nunez, they maintained a loving relationship.

'I was with Cristina Yesterday the then President, perhaps to annoy said.

To which Miriam would have answered, spiteful:

- Oh yeah? Do you know who I was? I had coffee with Miguel Nunez.

- With Nunez?

- Yes, to discuss the Government's communication strategy ... Between us, do not know how you have that kind of spokesman who betrayed you with your wife.

Kirchner's face turned red. Was there really been any relationship between the spokesman and Cristina? Or Quiroga just have sought revenge for the previous comment from your boss?

The truth is that Nunez, before being the government spokesman, had played the same role alongside Kirchner's wife in the '90s, when she held successive seats of deputy and senator in Buenos Aires, away from Santa Cruz.

A spokesman says former friend ever heard to comment that fueled the misunderstanding says once said that Cristina had eating out of his hand.

The only person who could confirm it is the Núñez himself, but he did not: despite working as spokesman, he is famous for not talking to the press.

His career in government ended some time after the talk between Kirchner and Miriam Quiroga, in mid-2009, when former president spent above the President and decided it needed a new official spokesman. The choice was Alfredo Scoccimarro, Cork, who was kept at a safe distance from Cristina.

Capitanish

When a reporter asked what his relationship with the President, Jorge Capitanich (49 years) knot loosened his tie as if gasping for air. "We are good friends ... Sometimes we share a mate (mate tea)," the governor of the province of Chaco blushed. The reporter did not understand why the challenged acted like a teenager caught at fault.

"I just wanted you to find out the degree of political affinity that existed between the two. I had no idea the rumors circulating around Capitanich and Cristina Kirchner," he said, when he had blundered thoroughly.

But this interview is nothing, compared to what happened during the patriotic celebrations of May 25, 2011, where a woman with tousled hair advanced hurling insults to the stage where Jorge Capitanich and his guest, Cristina Fernandez de Kirchner, presided the ceremony. The bodyguards failed to stop it.

The governor's wife, Sandra Mendoza approached the President and was a good time whispering in his ear who knows what, for fear of competition.

The result was the guest of honor was made a

statue for the rest of the act. "Mendoza was sick with jealousy as three days before this scandal, her husband had returned from New York where along with the head of the Government had been participating in the Summit of the UN" and one of the bodyguards surprised the governor entering late night at Four Seasons, the hotel where Cristina was staying.

The then head of the State Intelligence Service (SIDE), Miguel Angel Toma, even took note of this report. It was not his job to interfere in the private life of Mrs. President.

But somehow, the episode reached the ears of Mendoza, who already suspected that her husband and the tenant of the Casa Rosada shared more than infusions of mate and it seems that it informed the President.

Ivan Heyn

Another romances attributed to Cristina had a much more abrupt end. Ivan Heyn (35 years) had a close friendship with Maximo Kirchner, the eldest son of the president and now the most influential person within his inner circle. On the recommendation of Maximus, the professional who graduated with honors from the University of Buenos Aires and member of La Campora, the youth wing of kirchnerismo, whence come many of the brains that today the country was administered.

During the presidency of Nestor Kirchner, Ivan

Heyn served as advisor to the finance ministers and Miguel Peirano Felisa Miceli. Previously, he worked at the Ministry of Industry, Trade and SMEs as a specialist in production and sector development issues. Already under President Cristina Fernandez de Kirchner, between May 2008 and January 2009 he was Secretary of Industry, with Carlos Fernandez as economy minister. Between January 2009 and January 2011 he served as manager of macroeconomic and sectoral studies Bank for Investment and Foreign Trade (BICE).

In 2010 he was appointed chairman of the Corporation Antiguo Puerto Madero SA, in charge of urban development of Buenos Aires neighborhood of Puerto Madero, representing the national government. In February 2011 he was also appointed to the board of the company Aluar, one of the largest aluminum producers in South America, representing the share capital held by the National Administration of Social Security (ANSES).

In the legislative elections of the City of Buenos Aires 2011 Heyn was a candidate for the list of the Front for Victory (FPV), the coalition government of President Fernandez de Kirchner, although in a position considered testimonial. He also was part of the advisory team of Daniel Filmus, candidate for head of government of the City by the FPV, who would be defeated in the second round by the conservative Mauricio Macri.

On December 10, 2011, assuming Cristina Fernandez de Kirchner his second term, he was appointed Undersecretary of Foreign Trade and International Relations of the Ministry of Economy and Public Finance, a position newly created.

And it is that Cristina Fernandez de Kirchner seems to have grown fond of young talent and the relationship maintained have been known for intimate family circles and even the president is said to have commented before the death of her husband.

Ten days later, after forcing the1062 room door at the Radisson Montevideo hotel, the guards found the lifeless body of a young man hanged with a belt hanging closet.

But having found no signs of violence, it was thought that the Undersecretary of Foreign Trade of Argentina had taken his own life after participating in foreign "sex games" and when the president learned of the tragedy, suffered a concussion and had to receive care medical. After it was rumored that the president had an intense affair with a senior officer of the Federal Police, especially after the tribute that surrendered a day after his death.

"I remember this as a young man, 'economist street' as he liked to be called, as they called their peers. It was our secretary ofForeign tradeIvan Heyn. "

"A young man of many who joined politics.

Had onehistoryI always commented. itsfatherproduct of the crisis of 2000-2001 merged company strapsforcars. "

"From being a 'good boy', as some would say, upper middle class, had to make a living fighting it because his family left the country and is still outside the country." But he decided to stay in his country. He continued his studies and making pulseritas the pension was paid. He finished the race and it was a brilliant economist. "

"He was a tireless campaigner," added the president who confessed that knowing the Newsran out of air. "Yesterday I ran out of air, because young people I see them as my children, because besides Ivan had the same age as my son, 34 years."

Accidental death

The case in which the death of Undersecretary of Foreign Trade, Ivan Heyn, which occurred in December 2012 in the Uruguayan capital while participating in the Mercosur Summit with President Cristina Fernandez, was closed two months later branded as "accident was investigated ".

This was confirmed by the press officer of the Montevideo Police, commissioner José Luis Rondán inspector Godoy, who explained that "the case is closed because all possibilities are exhausted tests".

"It closes as an accident," said Godoy Rondán referring to the cause Heyn, who on December 20 last was found hanging in the hotel room where the delegation was staying Argentina during the Mercosur Summit.

At first it was thought that Heyn, 34, leader of La Campora, had committed suicide because he had a belt around his neck tied to the bar of a closet, but researchers were directed to it was an accident when the staff practiced extreme masturbation, consisting climax at the edge of asphyxiation, the alleged purpose of enhancing the pleasure. On this subject, the general commissioner, speaking to Radio La Red, admitted that "it was handled and what the coroner had already advanced some of that and indeed on the right track with respect to that hypothesis."

"Made the relevant expertise and investigations, the judge (Homer Da Costa) understood that they had exhausted all means in order to determine the possibility that someone else may have been involved in this event," said the police.

The relationship with Judge Garzón

Baltasar Garzon has been established in Argentina since he disable from office in February 2012 under the instruction of the Gürtel case, one case of most notorious corruption in Spain and that, for now, it would have been convicted .

No wonder that Garzón take Argentina as a country girl when after having felt slighted by the Spanish legal and political system after the conviction for illegal wiretapping in Gürtel, because in the austral country has always defended the Andalusian judge as "a world example "and it has enjoyed since he tried to prosecute César Augusto Pinochet enormous popularity as reflected in that la president of Argentina, Cristina Fernandez de Kirchner, on December 11, 2010 is nt the pageantry and stars of just causes to hold a rally in defense of human rights in the legendary Plaza de Mayo in Buenos Aires, the then assumed the starting point of its policy toward the presidential election race. A race in which the President would have the support of his personal friend, Baltasar Garzon.

Many guests were stunned by the appearance of the hotel reception Park Tower in Buenos Aires, the Sheraton chain, the Spanish judge who was recently suspended by the Spanish judiciary. Dressed in immaculate summery outfit, peopled hair graying after recent disappointments and yet, with a few extra kilos, Garzon traveler landed in Argentina to support the widow president and, incidentally, be honored for his work on behalf "truth and justice".

Among effusive hugs and greetings, the magistrate was the star in the lobby of the Park Tower, a scenario that merged, as can only be done in Latin America, the colorful indigenismo, professionals claim rights of others and the local political establishment. All this, though, against the backdrop of the towering marble columns and piano music of an exceptional luxury hotel.

Far from reproach, punishment and dishonorable expatriation to suffer at the hands of his countrymen, global vigilante is an institution in Argentina, as was once again revealed. In a ceremony scheduled as a festive marathon, Garzón starred with Fito Paez and hip-hop group Calle 13, which used the event to present his latest album.

Garzón at the event shared award, at least, with other celebrities of matter, such as specialized human rights lawyer Martin Luther King III and German Beate Klarsfeld, famous for its catches of hidden Nazi criminals in Latin America after the Second World War.

And besides, is his long career in defense of human rights, which led him to have a special "tune" with the Argentine government characterized, from the presidency of the late Nestor Kirchner, for making historical memory one of their banners, by which it did not surprise many that from this disqualification in Spain Garzón decided to "exile" in the Latin American country.

But the former judge Baltasar Garzon relationship with Argentina now takes other more romantic overtones; Since the president of Argentina, Cristina Fernandez de Kirchner, and he will surpass the mere common interest in recovering the historical memory of both boast.According to a Mexican magazine "Who" published in March 2013, the president of Argentina, Cristina Fernandez de Kirchner, and former Spanish judge Baltasar Garzon, maintain an intense romance and secret. Or rather, almost secret, as holding a growing out of the halls of the Casa Rosada version.

And is that according to the article by Veronica Calderon, contrasted with Spanish sources and not just media or contrary journalists the president as the Clarin group, jienense lawyer married to Rosario Molina, has been one of the most frequent guests of Cristina and 'encounter' of two such strong personalities has emerged an instant passion, which, however, the medium can not confirm if has endured and continues romance.

For Baltasar Garzón has earned a reputation for being "very lapdog" and has not only maintained a relationship that both the magazine and the journalist qualifies as the most intense, the most famous widow of Argentina, but also with a Brazilian and Colombian and how the old 'court star' has taken up residence in Argentina, after rumors that there may be a relationship with the South American head of state have grown. In fact, 'Who', the Mexican magazine has revealed the romance and sells 82,000 copies of his biweekly, ensures that the sparks of passion arose when the lawyer was the guest of honor at the inauguration of Fernandez in December 2.011 and since then, it has become a frequent events of the Presidency in fact, was the one who gave his Argentine identity card last November, "they conclude in the Aztec publication wizard.

The Spanish judge who ordered the arrest of the dictator Augusto Pinochet dismantled the network of ETA and recently declared himself dealing with the defense of Wikileaks founder

Julian Assange, occupy, since shortly after his conviction in Spain, the post of advisor the Commission on Human Rights of the Argentine Parliament, Kirchner managed by Remo Carlotto, which it was not particularly well received by the opposition and his name has also sounded to be one of the directors of the truth commission studying the agreement between Argentina and Iran in the AMIA bombing in 1994.

The judge who has a residence permit for one year in Argentina, andit has been active in various acts of kirchnerismo, being one of the most remarkable defense of judicial reform by the government of his "lover" or the third trial on ESMA, which the also adviser to the International Criminal Court in The Hague had appeared among the public, hours before delivering their residence permit during the second session of the third trial on the crimes committed by the last dictatorship in Argentina (1976-1983) at the School Navy mechanical (ESMA), one of the largest secret detention centers regime.

"After Nuremberg, I do not think there has been a trial of this magnitude for crimes against humanity. That is very important not only for Argentina but for the whole world, "said Garzon told reporters.

The third trial on the ESMA is the greatest of all proceedings initiated against state terrorism in Argentina by the number of defendants, about 68, that of court offenses, some 789, and witnesses, nearly 900, will parade to over two years for the courtrooms. Among the 68 defendants include some of the former military and Argentine former police Garzon pursued in the 90s of the last century and early this century, under the criteria of universal justice and when in the South American country still ruled amnesties that were abolished in Government Nestor Kirchner (2003-2007).

Garzón was on a balcony that has the courtroom. On the giant screen installed there you could see the faces of the accused, but they could not watch him. "For me, [this act] is to meet again with the faces of many of those in Spain investigated, especially Ricardo Cavallo. Many of those here were processed by me, and watch them on trial is what any judge sucks, especially as serious as these facts. That [the trial] is being done in Argentina is a win for everyone and especially for the victims, "concluded the exjuez.

Garzon came to trial in the company of the president of Grandmothers of Plaza de Mayo, Estela de Carlotto, who is still looking for hundreds of babies disappeared born in captivity and were handed over to then members of the security forces or persons associated with them .

In recent months,the former judge had also received honors in several cities in Argentina. He had also met with several politicians and some measures backed government of Fernandez, the law on audiovisual media concentration or the fight against litigating creditors by the bankruptcy of Argentina in 2001.

It has also supported, for example, the judge of Jujuy (Northwest South American country) who prosecuted one of the most powerful businessmen in Argentina, Carlos Pedro Blaquier, for alleged collaboration in crimes of the dictatorship.

During the ceremony permit the President of Argentina praised, amid applause from the audience at the Casa Rosada, the exjuez as follows: "Baltasar Garzón has made us the honor to request his residence here, in Argentina, and also as a representative of a justice that is not only of human rights linked to the terrible dictatorships that ravaged our country, but speaks of the human rights of second, third, fourth, fifth generation, as they call it, and that I would summarize in the right to live with hope and illusion. "

The magazine article Who is only one page and takes three pictures where you see them together, but all are taken from public events, even one of them is 2.005, while he was still alive Nestor Kirchner, so it is not easy to find photographic evidence of this romance that, according to the magazine, was the talk in the areas where moved until recently the famous jurist in Spain. From the Casa Rosada they have not denied this information, and although a statement from the Casa Rosada expected, this three months later has not occurred.

However, photographic evidence and even videos are there. The kichnerismo has tried to get rid of them by all possible means, but we have them and I offer them exclusively.

The growing wealth of the relatives of the Kirchner government

secretaries enriched

In the case of the Argentine government, the saying is true: "who snuggles up to good tree, good shade shelters him." It is a long list that make politicians and officials who have enriched themselves after having approached the Kirchners. We analyze the most famous names.

Illicit enrichment of the closest marriage politicians and officials no longer a secret when Argentine journalist Jorge Ernesto Lanata, known for writing in the newspaper Clarin and other publisher profile, presented its heritage in its' Periodismo para todos '.

We review the most prominent cases focusing on the following figures:

Daniel Muñoz

It was the private secretary of Nestor Kirchner, in the years of his term as in the first two years of President Cristina. He was in charge of attending Nestor throughout, and was the person with whom everyone previously spoke before to contact the president. When Muñoz became part of kirchnerista circle, just he had a Volkswagen Golf '99 and presidential secretary salary; when he left office in 2009, owned land in Mar de las Pampas of 675 square meters, another in El Calafate of 1,285 square meters, a model car Ford Focus 2006 and 430,000 pesos in your account. He currently lives in a home that exceeds 1,000 square meters, in addition to being located in one of the best areas in the neighborhood of Saavedra.

Fabian Gutierrez

It was the personal secretary Cristina, although he began working for Nestor. With this, he was appointed deputy secretary, but notable for being the companion Cristina in his political career. In 2003, his estate was 58,636 pesos; in just five years, this was sevenfold, from 402,392 pesos. Although it may seem that it was the faithful friend of Cristina, in 2005 he resigned because "I could not stand more crazy."

Ricardo Echegaray

Lawyer and politician, as well as official, in December 2008 joined the staff of Cristina as head of the Federal Administration of Public Revenue (AFIP), the body that controls national tax collection. In 2003 he declared a total of 159,700 pesos, which rose up to 3,764,911 pesos in 2011. In addition, your home is valued at nearly two million pesos, plus two more apartments he owns, and enjoy three cars and two boats vehicles valued at nearly 500,000 pesos.

Ricardo Barreiro

The gardener and caretaker of the house of

Kirchner in El Calafate, Barreiro walked quickly into the closest of friends of the couple circle. He was also secretary of Nestor, and now a hotelier and restaurateur. In its heritage, it has a cottage complex in El Calafate, as well as a hotel called Altos de Amaicha, considered one of the most prestigious place. In addition, he is the father of Pablo Barreiro, today's personal secretary Cristina.

Rudy Ulloa

Currently businessman, was the personal assistant of Nestor and his driver. Upward mobility in the shade of the Kirchner marriage was undeniable, so that has come to declare "not forgive me success" as a defense to charges of money laundering. Currently it owns a mansion in Río Gallegos, manages two audiovisual production companies and enjoys nine high-end cars. In addition, habitual residence is a luxury house in Las Lomas de San Isidro, Buenos Aires exclusive area, which acquired for $ 700,000.

The vault in the chalet Calafate

Thanks to the statements of the former secretary and lover, the late President Nestor Kirchner, we know that several of the bags of money that came from the Casa Rosada would stop building the house of El Calafate.

Clear enrichment of the Kirchner family in such a short time, was the subject of rumors and slanders against them, arguing that the money came from taxes that everyone contributes in Argentina region.

So much so that now, after 3 years of the president's death, his secretary has revealed many of the best kept secrets Kirchner and one of them was the phone conversation with the alleged builder of the property in El Calafate.

"He demanded to advance faster in the construction of the vaults. This is what I heard. There are large doors, armored doors" were the words that Quiroga was able to hear in the next office to the president, which was situated yours.

The estate was acquired El Calafate in 2005, when they buy 60,000 m2 on three grounds, without selling any goods which had so far. Arriving to accumulate 28 properties for the farm the following year pocketing a profit by selling land purchased one of 6,000 m2. They invested heavily in the construction of huts on these grounds close to $ 270,000 in the cabins, but the money was achieved by renting them, reaching 472,314 dollars to repay registered.

Now all the "dead" businesses that had made her husband, question whether Cristina knew about all of them, what Secretary of Kirchner stated flatly "I can assure you that he was aware of everything."

Investigations into the alleged crimes of corruption both husband of Cristina own remain in the hands of judges who will decide at all times which is the punishment for all these accusations fall on the president.

Ex-lover confesses about moneybags

Miriam Quiroga, the renowned ex-lover of the president, confessed to the media have seen Kirchner with moneybags.

The big unknown for all, Secretary of the dead president, Kirchner knew since 1990 and continued with him until the time of his death. It was one of the people their utmost confidence to revealing each and every one of its secrets. So much so he came to make her his mistress.

Quiroga confessed that he had left everything for him, his family, his home, everything, and decided to move from the south to be with Nestor. He never left him alone, even on his first trip as president, she went to all the tour performing around the country.

When he came to power, Kirchner did not

hesitate a second upload category and place it in the Directorate of Documentation of Presidency of the Nation, where they often receive and answer all letters sent to the Government House and are directed to whom It occupies the presidency of Argentina.

In 2010,Quiroga attempted a political space which gained notoriety minimal, leading the creation of the "National Project", a called "Peronist space" aligned kirchnerismo, designed to work on the possible candidacy for president Nestor Kirchnerin 2011.

Quiroga continued its firm position until the death of the president and the rise to power of his wife Cristina Fernandez, who, influenced by Oscar Parrilli which told the romance between her husband and the secretary, sought the perfect excuse to fire her from office. He disguised himself as a ceded his post to Mariana Larroque, sister Andrés Larroque, friend Max Kirchner and secretary general of the group La Campora, a group that grew after the influence of the son of Cristina, Maximus in the second term of the President.

But former Secretary of the Argentine president was not going to sit idly by after losing his job and saw an opportunity to speak to the media to clarify their entire relationship with Kirchner. "It is common knowledge that I was Kirchner's lover. We had a very strong union, "declared Quiroga media and journalists trustworthy.

However, fear of Cristina was not to give these statements, as was well known, if not for a compelling things about her husband that were not true, or at least Cristina did not know them, but seeing the situation they were living was He was defeated by meeting her husband. But that day came, and Quiroga made an interview in which he unveiled each and every one of the secrets that the former president had saved his best drawer.

In the "Journalism for All" Jorge Lanata, former Secretary television program Kirchner declared that what she saw on the money bags that allegedly contained money. "A year after Nestor came to power they began arriving at the Casa Rosada, a full black sacks of cash. Then, silver was transferred to Santa Cruz in the presidential plane" declared Quiroga to the media, who accused Daniel Muñoz (secretary of Kirchner) to perform this process.

After his remarks, the cause that had opened in 2008 after several complaints of the deputy Elisa Carrio for president of the Argentine government when Kirchner was at the head, was reactivated by the federal judge Luis Rodriguez. Carrió asked to be investigated for alleged conspiracy to former President Kirchner, several of its officers, Julio De Vido, Ricardo Jaime and Claudio Uberti, and some businessmen, like Lazarus Baez and Christopher Lee, who Quiroga also named in his interview . Kirchner is presumed to be treasured "dirty money" from the alleged commissions charged Báez, in one of the houses owned by the family in the town of El Calafate.

Following these statements, Elisa Carrio filed in federal court testimony Quiroga, delivering a copy of the television program and declared "Quiroga told exactly what I related the Prosecutor and the Judge in 2008, hopefully now the judge Ercolini by so check the cause. " In addition, the federal judge Julian Ercolini quoted Quiroga to declare before a court on statements that poured into the television accusing the secretary Muñoz carried bags with money.

Meanwhile, Carrio continues its constant struggle to dismantle the government for so many years deceived the Argentine people, and will not stop until its purpose, and less with current statements of Quiroga and previous Fariña, who in the same program secretary, he assumed his participation as Báez right hand and explained that the financial network was composed of more than 50 false corporations through which the black money would stop to accounts abroad.

Blood stained hands

Relations with drug trafficking are not the only murky issue that was related to President Kirchner. In 2010, both Cristina and Máximo Kirchner, wife and son of Nestor Kirchner, are accused of killing the former president of a shot in the neck.

The event of the death of former Argentine leader becomes controversial on 9 May this 2013 due to a complaint filed by the lawyer and politician Juan Ricardo Mussa, in which he accused the president and his son had committed murder Nestor Kirchner. In the legal text, published in the Argentine newspaper Perfil, referring to two witnesses who allegedly witnessed the atrocious event it was well.

In the lawsuit, Mussa asked to Kirchner's body

exhumed to check if the version of witnesses, those mentioned in the document that would have been "killed by a shot in the neck during a heated discussion of marriage," agrees. In addition to that request, the political requests that several businessmen investigation by covering up the crime, those related to illegal bleaching capital and payment of commissions to Nestor in exchange for contracts. Finally, it also requires the attendance of the doctors who treated Nestor Kirchner at his home in his alleged illness that preceded his death.

The official version of the death of Nestor Kirchner

The death certificate of the former president was signed on 27 October 2010 by the Medical Unit President. In it, it appears to cause fulminant death from cardiovascular deficiencies infarction; the former president had previously suffered heart problems that led him to the hospital in the past, being involved on September 12, 2010, day when he underwent an angioplasty. Kirchner had suffered cardiac arrest early in the morning of 27 at his home in Calafate. Subsequently, the wake was held with the closed casket, so it is unknown whether the attested version could be true.

ABOUT THE AUTHOR

Director of mil21.es newspaper journalist.
Collaborating opinion of a dozen online
publications. He was director of the newspaper La
Cronica in Almería for 17 years from 1982. He
worked in newsrooms de Arriba, El Alcázar, Diario
de Avisos, People, Pyresa agency, etc. He directed
the weekly El Caso and today is CEO of Cibeles
Group, LLC.

Made in the USA
Middletown, DE
05 May 2022

65295709R00082